# The Lost Child

*A story of recovery from Narcissitic Abuse*

# The Lost Child

*A story of recovery from Narcissistic Abuse*

## Charlie Blakely

**Kindle Direct Publishing - Amazon**

Copyright © 2023 Charlie Blakely

All rights reserved

No part of this book may be reproduced, or stored in a retrieval system, or transmitted in any form or by any means, electronic, mechanical, photocopying, recording, or otherwise, without express written permission of the publisher.

ISBN-9798378160341

Cover design by: Benjamin Bajeux and Buzbooks

Printed in the United Kingdom

*This book is dedicated to my brother, The Mother's scapegoat.
Sadly he left this world still traumatised by his childhood.*

*ACKNOWLEDGEMENTS:*

*To The Mother's ex friend Ann Keene, for being the only adult to show me physical affection growing up*

*To my drama teacher, Mr. Hart. The only adult who believed in me when I was at school*

*To my therapists, Lizz Ross and Benita Scott, who helped me to recovery from my childhood trauma*

*To Lauren Grant, who gave me the idea of self-publishing*

*To my friend Laura and colleague Matt, who gave me honest feedback both on a personal and professional level*

*To my sister and sister-in-law, Caroline and Susan Allett, who gave me treasured personal feedback*

*To Cath Humphrey, who not only gave me valuable feedback, but also generously acted as a free editor*

*To Benjamin Bajeux, who has designed the cover*

*To Sindy Suntharamoorthy, wo kindly acted as a free proof reader*

*To my ex-partner, who was a constant source of support for 15 years*

*Lastly and ironically I suppose, I would like to thank The Mother. Without her, there would be no book*

# Contents

Title Page
Title Page
Copyright
Dedication
Dedication
Disclaimer ..... 1
Introduction ..... 3
Chapter 1 - The Original Trauma ..... 8
Chapter 2 - Positive Narcissistic Supply ..... 10
Chapter 3 - The toddler years ..... 12
Chapter 4 - Mirroring ..... 14
Chapter 5 - Emotional Flashbacks ..... 16
Chapter 6 - Flying Monkeys ..... 18
Chapter 7 - Withholding ..... 23
Chapter 8 - Disassociation ..... 25
Chapter 9 - Breadcrumbing ..... 27
Chapter 10 - Trauma induced by others ..... 30
Chapter 11 - Narcissists are poor care takers ..... 34
Chapter 12 - Emotional Work ..... 38
Chapter 13 - Another frame of reference ..... 40

| | |
|---|---|
| Chapter 14 - Coercive Control | 43 |
| Chapter 15 - Narcissists don't grieve like others | 45 |
| Chapter 16 - Crocodile tears | 47 |
| Chapter 17 - Guilt | 50 |
| Chapter 18 - Narcissists isolate their victims | 52 |
| Chapter 19 - Narcissists are horrible gift-givers, unless they're 'love bombing' | 55 |
| Chapter 20 - The Silent Treatment | 57 |
| Chapter 21 - The narcissist's victim persona | 59 |
| Chapter 22 - Narcissists have superficial relationships | 61 |
| Chapter 23 - Puberty threatens the narcissist | 64 |
| Chapter 24 - The narcissist needs their victim to think they're stupid | 68 |
| Chapter 25 - The narcissist sees what they want to see | 72 |
| Chapter 26 - The narcissist lacks empathy | 75 |
| Chapter 27 - The narcissist's obsession with physical appearance | 79 |
| Chapter 28 - Fictitious Disorder Imposed On Another (FDIA) | 83 |
| Chapter 29 - Narcissists are bullies | 87 |
| Chapter 30 - Narcissists are envious | 89 |
| Chapter 31 - My saving grace | 92 |
| Chapter 32 - Narcissists minimise our accomplishments | 96 |
| Chapter 33 - The narcissist abandons, despite this being their greatest fear | 99 |
| Chapter 34 - Narcissists sabotage their victim's success | 102 |
| Chapter 35 - The narcissist's ever-changing script | 105 |
| Chapter 36 - 'You can fuck off out of here when you're 16'...... | 108 |

| | |
|---|---|
| Chapter 37 - Freedom wasn't what I thought it would be | 113 |
| Chapter 38 - Co-dependency | 115 |
| Chapter 39 - Self-abandonment | 117 |
| Chapter 40 - Narcissists invent reasons to punish their victim | 122 |
| Chapter 41 - The narcissist flatters in order to gain control | 125 |
| Chapter 42 - Awakening happens in stages | 130 |
| Chapter 43 - From Lost Child to Golden Child | 134 |
| Chapter 44 - Repetition Compulsion | 142 |
| Chapter 45 - The road to recovery | 146 |
| Chapter 46 - Life changing epiphanies | 151 |
| Chapter 47 - Courage repels narcissists | 157 |
| Chapter 48 - Special Occasions | 162 |
| Chapter 49 - Going 'No contact' | 175 |
| Chapter 50 - Complex Post Traumatic Stress Disorder (CPTSD) | 181 |
| Chapter 51 - Moving On | 186 |
| Chapter 52 - Recovery tools and tips | 192 |
| | 199 |

# Disclaimer

Although I am a mental health worker, I do not claim to be a professional. This is simply my story of recovery from narcissistic abuse. Which was enabled by my understanding of the issue based on my lived experience, research, and work experience in the field of mental health.

CHARLIE BLAKELY

# Introduction

This is a book of hope and recovery from Complex Post Traumatic Stress Disorder (CPTSD), induced by narcissistic parenting. I believe my mother to have Narcissistic Personality Disorder (NPD). I've listed the nine diagnosable traits found in the DSM-V (Diagnostic and Statistical Manual, 5th edition) at the end of 'Going No Contact'- Chapter 49.

It's because of her disorder that I do not, and never have had an emotional connection with her, despite my best efforts. Because of this lack of attachment, I refer to her as "The Mother" throughout.

I have siblings whose coping strategies and survival skills differ from mine. They rarely seemed to find discussing details from the past therapeutic. Therefore, I've written under a pseudonym to protect their identities.

XXX

Long-term victims of narcissism often suffer from cognitive dissonance - believing in two opposing thoughts simultaneously. Despite the evidence, we tend to believe what the narcissist says. This confused state is often induced by 'gaslighting' - the attempt to deliberately confuse another person's perception of reality.

Living with cognitive dissonance daily causes a kind of 'brain fog.' For me, this led to the classic 'freeze' response—psychological, emotional, and sometimes physical paralysis. My reaction to abuse was often to say and do nothing because I often felt nothing. I was numb and in a disassociated state for much of my life.

Because of the brain fog, my memories are fragmented, which means that sometimes I remember what was said but not where we were, for example. Or I remember where we were, but not what was said, etc. I've chosen not to embellish for the sake of storytelling, because remaining authentic has always been a significant part of my healing journey. I hope I can be forgiven for my occasional abrupt endings or glossed-over details of recollections.

XXX

Narcissistic parents tend to force roles onto their children to maintain control in the household. There is almost always the dichotomy between the Golden Child (the favoured one, who usually gets more expensive gifts, and more freedom); and the Scapegoat, the child who typically gets blamed for everything. However, if there are more children in the family, there is room for the Hero, the child (usually older) who tries to present the family as normal to the rest of the world, and the Lost/Invisible Child, the one who is mainly ignored.

The purpose of these roles is to 'divide and conquer'. If the children have no loyalty to each other or trust amongst each other, it's easier for the narcissistic parent to continue their abuse, unabated. These roles are usually fixed. However, if the narcissistic parent believes that it will benefit them, they can change these roles at will.

XXX

Responses to abuse can be neatly compartmentalised into what Pete Walker calls 'the 4 F's'. 'Fight, Flight, Freeze, and

Fawn.'

As a young child, I witnessed how much the scapegoat was hated for fighting back. This paralysed my 'fight' response early on.

I ran away once, but this only made matters worse. So that paralysed my 'flight' response. So, I gravitated toward the 'freeze response' for much of my life. From my late 20s to mid-30s, I 'fawned' over The Mother, hoping that if I showered her with gifts and attention, she would reciprocate and give me the love I longed for. But it all fell flat. How we respond to our trauma is linked to the Child Role imposed upon us.

I resembled the Lost Child most closely. I retreated into myself. Feeling invisible most of the time. When loving a narcissist, there is rarely any return on our emotional investment (and when there is, we usually discover the return to be hollow.)

I eventually began to fight back at 34 years old. Once I'd figured out that freezing, fleeing, and fawning didn't work, I took on parenting her. (Narcissists often 'parentify' their children) – The classic role reversal. I felt that if I could model love, understanding, and respect, she would be able to follow suit. But the happier, the more independent, and the more confident I grew, the more difficult she became. Realising that she was angry at my happiness was the portal to awakening – eventually resulting in going no contact. I've been in recovery from narcissistic abuse for the past 11 years and am now ready to share my story.

XXX

I discovered narcissism during a bit of downtime at work, in my previous profession as a teacher. It was towards the end of the school year. Exams were over, and I found myself alone in my room at my computer. Having had many upsetting encounters with The Mother, I decided to do some research. I typed 'What's wrong with my mother?' into a search engine, and up popped a variety of personality disorders, none of which I had heard of.

Within about five minutes, I came across the term Narcissistic Personality Disorder. It was a light bulb moment. I said out loud, 'Oh my God! Oh my God!! Oh my God!!! It's not me! It's her!!' There was a sudden realisation that I had done nothing wrong all these years.

Of course, we are all a product of our upbringing, and The Mother was no different. She was raised in a house where her basic needs were not met. There was inadequate heating, food, clothing, and frequent physical and verbal abuse. If she had been born today, all the children in the family would most likely have been taken into care. Aside from her basic needs not being met, she was also deprived of an education, treated like a slave from the age of 12, and probably, and more importantly, she never knew love, kindness, or affection. It is my belief she developed a personality disorder because of this unresolved childhood trauma.

Narcissists can create second-generation narcissists. I believe that is usually the golden child. I suspect this because they sense that their better treatment does not come from love. I think the golden child has some awareness that they are being used and pitted against their siblings, but it is hard for them to resist the parent's narrative because they come out on top. They are invested in colluding with the narcissist. So, they accept their better treatment, however shallow and insincere. They buy into the narrative that they are better than their siblings because it is their best option.

XXX

Again, I would like to add the disclaimer that my knowledge of narcissism is based on my personal experience, research, and work as a mental health support worker. We are learning all the time. So, everything I've written at the time of going to print is what I know or believe to be true now. No doubt, some of this will change in time with further research.

I'm based in the UK, where we have an NHS (National Health Service). So, some suggestions for recovery at the end of the book pertain to the UK only.

I hope this book reaches anyone who feels they were not loved as a child. Or anyone who feels they've been in a toxic relationship. It can, I believe, be used as an aid to support mental health recovery.

Although I write in an autobiographical style, my story is only important in so much that it conveys relevant information for those recovering from parental narcissistic abuse. Therefore, this is more of a self-help book than a literary masterpiece.

***Personality Disorder*** - *a mental disorder that gives a person a rigid and unhealthy set of thinking patterns and behaviours, which makes it difficult for them to maintain healthy relationships.**

# Chapter 1 – The Original Trauma

I'm standing at the top of the stairs in my nightie. My parents are at the bottom of the stairs standing near the front door. They are whispering. I don't know why I'm standing at the top of the stairs. Its' possible there was shouting earlier, and it woke me out of my sleep.

I'm upset. Dad suddenly notices me. He looks up. I know he's about to leave the house for the last time. I can't explain how I know. I just do. I don't want my dad to go. I'm crying, panicking and distraught…..

Suddenly, I'm at the bottom of the stairs. Crying hysterically. I'm hurt physically now. I don't remember how I got here. I either tripped in my attempt to stop him from leaving. Or I threw myself down the stairs so that he wouldn't go.

I look up to him, trying desperately to communicate in my two-year-old way, 'Dad, please don't leave. Please don't leave me with *her*!'

He bends down to comfort me. He calmly and gently rubs my arm… But then he gets up and leaves quietly, despite my protestation and tears.

I look up to the only adult available to give me comfort. She looks down at me with her arms folded contemptuously. Her eyes communicate, 'What are *you* so upset for? It's not you he's leaving; it's *me*! It's me who should be upset!'

I look up into her eyes. Scanning them for something. Reassurance? Compassion? She's offended by my display of emotion for my dad. Perhaps seeing it as a betrayal. Her contorted expression shows a demand for unquestioning loyalty. Somehow, through her micro-expressions, she's willing me to be angry with him on her behalf. Not cry after him.

Of course, I'm entirely incapable of the subliminal emotional demands placed on me. I know I've let her down. I feel like a failure.

XXX

It was only in my adult years that I recollected that she didn't move to comfort me when I ended up at the bottom of the stairs. She did not react to my pain. It didn't resonate with her. Instead, there was an air of silent hostility emanating from her, even as I was howling in physical pain and emotional distress.

XXX

I knew then, instinctively, that her reaction wasn't normal. I knew I wasn't safe with her, perhaps because her behaviour was in such contrast to my dad's. My terror at being left with her at two makes me wonder what I'd experienced at her hands before this moment.

Despite there being three other siblings in the house, I have no recollection of them being present. I've often questioned why I woke, yet siblings five or six years older than me didn't seem to hear the commotion. This is a question that's remained unanswered to this day.

***Original trauma** - There's usually one that all other traumas are borne out of. So, it's helpful to uncover what the original trauma is in therapy.*

# Chapter 2 - Positive Narcissistic Supply

The Mother occasionally reminisced about a particularly sunny day when I was a toddler in the pram. She seemed to enjoy telling this rather dull and pointless story.

I was wearing pearly white ankle socks and white shoes, apparently. She said people would stop in the street to compliment the contrast between the white socks and shoes and my tanned legs, the only visible part of me protruding from the pram.

Seemingly flattered by the attention I'd brought her, she felt kind enough to bestow a small portion of this 'supply' upon me. Her eyes dancing with glee and with a beaming smile, she recalled, in her broad Irish accent, "Sure, ye'd have the two little legs out!" She seemed to feed off this recycled, decades-old memory, in which I'd unwittingly brought her a sense of pride and joy.

I'd always felt odd, uneasy, and slightly embarrassed when she'd tell this story. Somehow, I was astute enough to know that the story was more about her than me, despite her best efforts to frame it as a compliment. Years later, I would understand why this story made me feel so uncomfortable. She was trying to flatter me. Flattery is one of the nine NPD traits.

XXX

As a result of this one incident, she developed an obsession with me getting a tan. But, try as she might, she never got that kind of 'positive narcissistic supply' again. No matter how many sunny days she locked me out in the garden in just my knickers.

I'd always remembered this as if it was a film clip. Looking at myself, rather than experiencing the memory as if it happened to me. This is disassociation, which will be discussed in Chapter 8.

Some narcissistic parents prefer positive narcissistic supply. They feed off their offspring's success rather than sabotage it.

*'**Supply**'- The emotional energy narcissists need from others to regulate their own emotions.*

# Chapter 3 - The toddler years

As a result of the original trauma, many problematic behaviours unravelled - symptoms of great inner turmoil. I had no hope of this turmoil ever being soothed or addressed with The Mother as the primary caregiver. With my dad as a buffer I believe I tolerated the coldness between us. Knowing that it wouldn't be long before his return, and I'd feel safe again. But without him as a buffer, I was emotionally starved.

Narcissists hold grudges and seek to punish like no one else. I believe my attachment to my dad sealed my fate there and then, the night of the original trauma.

The Mother would continue to show contempt for me frequently throughout my life, sometimes openly, sometimes subtly. But it was almost always there. Being too young to protect myself from her projections, I internalised her contempt for me. I believed myself to be fundamentally unlovable. Of course, my feelings were impossible to articulate as a toddler, but I felt and believed them, nonetheless.

It wasn't long before I developed self-harming habits to express my sense of loss and abandonment. I'd bang my head against walls, bite my arms and pull my hair out frequently. For some time after my dad left, I'd have 'melt-downs' in the street whenever I saw a car that looked like his.

The Mother had a multitude of stories regarding these years. All stored away, so she could regale others whenever the fancy took her. These stories were conveyed in a breezy, rehearsed monologue, oddly devoid of depth, concern, or compassion. In direct contrast to the content.

One story she'd regularly tell is regarding my distress at being left at nursery. I was, she said, always obviously distressed at being left, and attempted to escape daily by trying to climb the wire mesh fence that defined the perimeter of the nursery gardens. She'd cheerfully recall the 'funny' story of how I 'looked like a little monkey trying to escape.'

I was left at nursery every day, I believe, because she perceived my distress at being left as a sign of my love for her, rather than a fear of abandonment.

XXX

'The frozen baby experiment' proves that babies and toddlers feel emotional abandonment. It's available to find on YouTube.

https://youtu.be/YTTSXc6sARg

https://youtu.be/7Pcr1Rmr1rM


*Narcissists often behave in ways that elicit dramatic emotional responses from others. This narcissistic supply is what feeds their soul.*

## Chapter 4 - Mirroring

One day I unexpectedly spotted The Mother in the street as I was being walked home from nursery. The moment I saw her, I was overcome with pure, ecstatic joy. My heart filled with excitement as I ran towards her with my arms outstretched. Assuming she'd reciprocate and imagining she was happy to see me too, I charged toward her as fast as I could.

But, as I closed in on her, she remained upright, motionless, and expressionless. Still holding her shopping bags. When I got within earshot, she said stony-faced, "Sure, I thought ye was going to fall over." Her words alone could indicate concern if taken at face value, but there was no concern in her tone or face. My heart sank with disappointment and embarrassment. I corrected myself, mirroring her body language. I wiped the smile off my face and brought my hands down by my sides.

I was only about four, but even at the time, I knew that what she said was a pretence of concern. What lay beneath was clear. Contempt - for me, for showing affection so publicly, spontaneously, and unashamedly. She wanted to take the wind out of my sails, it seemed. Put me back in my place. And she certainly did that. I felt foolish, and made sure never to make this shameful mistake again.

XXX

An example of poor mirroring can be seen by Myka Stauffer, the YouTube family vlogger that became internet famous for 'rehoming' a special needs kid she adopted from China. There's a video of her daughter crying because Myka will be getting on a plane the following day without her. Instead of comforting her child, she enjoys positive narcissistic supply. She smirks at the camera and laughs playfully with her audience, amused by her daughter's distress.

***Mirroring** – Emotionally healthy parents instinctively mirror the expressions of their child. Narcissistic parents expect the child to mirror them.*

# Chapter 5 - Emotional Flashbacks

Up until the day we shopped for my first school uniform, her contempt for me seemed to be our private affair. This was the first time I felt publicly humiliated by her. Right there, on the shop floor, in full view of other shoppers, she roughly yanked down my trousers, without warning, exposing my knickers.

I squirmed, trying to pull my trousers back up, pointing to the dressing room, pleading, "It's just there!" I pleaded. She ignored my obvious embarrassment and knelt to force me into a school pinafore. Pushing it over my head and swearing at me under her breath to 'stop looking for attention!' (The irony!)

I could feel my cheeks burning. My bottom lip began to quiver, and my eyes filled with water. She was too angry to notice that I felt helpless, embarrassed, and betrayed by her for exposing me like this.

XXX

By the age of two, she'd exposed her contempt for me. By four, she'd revealed how incapable she was of affection. By the time I was five years old, I was very scared of her.

XXX

I've discovered through therapy that I've hated clothes shopping my whole life because the mere thought of it takes me back, emotionally, to this moment.

Emotional flashbacks are hard for others to recognise because it is such an internal experience. Often there are no clues for others to see. (I once got told that I was 'playing the victim' when I confided in someone, that I was experiencing an emotional flashback. Others can't comprehend the trauma inside us because we often don't demonstrate it outwardly.)

***'Emotional Flashback'*** *- When a current event triggers an emotional response to a past trauma. We're often unaware that we're experiencing an emotional flashback because they do not have a visual or auditory component like Post Traumatic Stress Disorder flashbacks.*

## Chapter 6 - Flying Monkeys

By the time I was of school age, I was extremely socially anxious. I was so fearful of others that the playground was a terrifying place for me to be. So, I avoided the playground, when others were in it and waited outside the school walls with The Mother, every morning; for the bell to ring. Class by class, all the children would eventually vacate the playground, making it safe for me to make my way into the building alone.

One day I must have gotten careless and forgotten myself. Perhaps I was caught up in a daydream (something I was prone to.) I allowed myself to be seen by a teacher.

Suddenly, I was shaken to the core by the hollering of my name into a bloody megaphone, no less! The whole school fell deafeningly silent, except my name, which was being screeched at full volume. "Charlie Blakely! I see you! Hiding behind that wall! Get yourself to the back of your line NOW!!"

I froze, hoping for some divine intervention……But nothing happened. Nothing, and no one was coming to rescue me. I had no choice.

I slowly made my way across the silent playground, with the eyes of the entire school on me, in what felt like a death march. My feet dragged, and my head hung in shame as my cheeks burned furiously. I was mortified.

On collecting me from school later that day, The Mother and I walked home with an even more awkward silent tension between us than usual. I wished she'd say something. I couldn't understand why she had nothing to say about my public humiliation that morning. She just willed the awkwardness away with her silence. I felt betrayed by her. Again.

XXX

I was mostly bored and frustrated in school and saw it as a necessary endurance test. Whilst many young people externalise their boredom and cause disruption, I was primarily quiet in class, preferring to daydream.

I was sent to a Catholic School, where teaching was not the priority. I spent countless mind-numbing hours and years sitting silently without knowing what the task was. I found no joy in anything. Every subject bored me.

I have a few recollections of teachers doing things that would be unthinkable today. But, because we children had no other frame of reference, we all took the unfair scoldings and arbitrary punishments compliantly. These incidents included frequent false accusations and public interrogations that often ended with physical assault.

The class was so used to these bully tactics that no one reacted to these instances, ever. It didn't occur to any of us to tell our parents. No one ever made fun of each other either, after these public trials. Not even in the playground afterwards. We silently sympathised with each other whilst feeling relief that it wasn't us that time, and fearful that it could be us next time. Even though we weren't all 'best buds,' there was a sense that we were all 'in it together.'

One particular teacher had a habit of poking us in the soft part of the shoulder with her long well-manicured fingernail. She liked to poke so hard that it was a challenge to maintain our balance. One time when I was on the receiving end of this abuse, she broke my skin, and blood seeped through my shirt.

The Mother later became friends with this woman's mother, knowing full well that her daughter had physically assaulted me numerous times. She had a way of aligning herself with others that treated me unkindly. (Narcissists are known for their lack of loyalty.)

Another typical behaviour of narcissists is to 'infantilise' their children by not teaching them self-care. I don't know if it's laziness, ineptitude, or a cruel plan to further isolate and ostracise their victim. (No child wants to be friends with the smelly kid!)

Either way, The Mother never showed me how to brush my teeth. Perhaps one day, someone commented on how bad my teeth were. Whatever the reason, I remember my first and only dental appointment as a child because it was such a strange and upsetting yet familiar experience.

She collected me from school early, refusing to tell me why or where we were going. Any attempt at eliciting information was stonewalled. We silently trudged along the street in the opposite direction from home. With me holding the buggy she was pushing, semi-jogging alongside her to keep up. We walked silently for what seemed like miles as I tried to read her demeanour. She seemed angry, but there was no indication of why.

Feet aching, we finally arrived at the dentist, who appeared to take an instant dislike to me, or perhaps she disliked all children. She seemed to believe that I was difficult. Repeating over and over, "If you co-operate with me, I'll co-operate with you." The dislike became mutual throughout the course of the appointment because there was a subtle threat underlying her mantra. I wasn't displaying any challenging behaviour and was silently obedient. Yet she continued to berate me as The Mother stood silent and still in the corner of the room, clasping her hands in front of her. Almost as if she was afraid of the dentist too.

She made me wear a gum shield with an orange-tasting gel inside it for what felt like a long time. I assume now to remove lots of built-up plaque. After the shield was removed, I was shown, for the very first time, how to brush my teeth by a patient young assistant, who wasn't anything at all like the miserable old bat who kept telling me to co-operate.

I was surprised at how long this teeth brushing business took, and kept stopping to ask, "Is that enough?" She kept saying "No" until it was. So, that was how I learned to brush my teeth.

XXX

Summers were often spent on the farmhouse in Ireland where The Mother was raised. She'd usually send us off for weeks in advance and then join us later. These 'holidays' were not fun. We were effectively dumped on relatives who barely knew us and had no interest in getting to know us.

In this environment, once again, her view of me was validated by most of my uncles and for no reason that I could see. As I said, they barely knew me, and I was not a demanding or challenging child. I learned how not to be a bother. In classic narcissistic style, I can only conclude that she drip-fed them negative stories about me over the years. Convincing other adults that I was a troublesome child made it difficult for me to develop a positive relationship with them.

I was too young to understand at the time. Still, I believe that every time I went to Ireland, I endured a 'smear campaign,' 'flying monkeys,' and 'triangulation' all simultaneously.

My uncles often triangulated me with my sister (using her to hurt me). They did this by treating her especially favourably whilst pointedly ignoring me. For example, one day, my younger sister got to leave the farm with my uncle and was bought sweets, on the proviso that she didn't tell me or share them with me. I knew that they were treating me, deliberately treating me unkindly, and I knew that I'd done nothing to deserve it.

I'm not sure how many summers we spent on that farm, but it was enough to significantly affect my sense of self. Like school, my time there felt like an endurance test. Knowing what I know now about the narcissist's use of 'triangulation' and 'the smear campaign,' I believe The Mother was responsible for how much the dentist, my teachers, and uncles seemed to dislike me.

Nothing else made sense. They all had the same opinion of me, which wasn't based on their personal experience of me.

Flying monkeys seldom know they are flying monkeys, and they don't know they are being used and lied to. They believe the victim is equally responsible for their difficulties with the narcissist, and wish we could all get along.

\***'Flying monkeys'** *fall for the subtle smear campaign run by the narcissist. And in doing so, they effectively continue the abuse. So, even when the narcissist isn't around, they're still in control of the narrative. They still get to abuse or neglect by proxy, through their flying monkeys.*

## Chapter 7 - Withholding

There was always an undercurrent of 'withholding' from The Mother. If I were a toy, I felt she'd have returned me to the shop for a refund. I definitely was not what she'd ordered when she'd asked the great cosmos for a child.

Before I started school at age five, I knew my feelings didn't matter to her. No matter how much I tried to express them, they were ignored. The logical conclusion I drew was that I was here to serve the needs of others. I believed, even at that age, that it was my job to make others feel better about themselves, particularly The Mother.

The first time I became aware of her withholding (although I didn't know there was a word for it) was on the long walks home from primary school. I was painfully aware of our silence, although she seemed oblivious.

I responded to this disconnection with quiet secret desperation. I felt responsible for the chasm between us and was compelled to fill it with the only thing I could think of. Tales of what had taken place for me that day. She never responded with interest, of course. But the sound of my voice provided me with temporary relief, a buffer. It was a distraction from the deafening silence of her painful disinterest.

Occasionally she would 'um' and 'ah' in the right places if I pressed for a reaction, but mostly she was pretty transparent about the fact that I was boring her.

Our brain plays funny tricks on us sometimes. By insisting on telling her about my day, I was, on some level, pretending that she was interested despite the evidence. In all those long walks home, she never once asked, 'How was your day?' or 'What did you learn in school today?' I longed to hear those words.

XXX

When I was about seven, she decided to enrol me in gymnastics. It wasn't long before a coach selected me. Very quickly, I was training every evening after school and travelling for competitions. Occasionally this involved long-distance travel and staying overnight with strangers. The Mother never asked for any details of those I stayed with. Of course, the coach caught on to this. So, it wasn't long before I stayed overnight at his house. She never asked for his address either.

Child abusers sense emotional deprivation in children. A counsellor told me once that a paedophile could walk into a room full of 30 kids and pick out the easiest to abuse in 30 seconds. That's precisely what happened, the day he walked into my gymnastics class and picked me out for his team.

Although her withholding of due care and attention led to abuse, my feelings around it were complicated. He was nicer to me than she was. If I'd had another frame of reference, I might have known I was being abused by him and neglected by her. But I didn't.

My siblings never seemed as bothered by her withholding as I was. It seemed they'd somehow managed to disconnect themselves from her emotionally.

*'**Withholding**' - This is more subtle than The Silent Treatment, but it still makes for uncomfortable and awkward interactions. With knowledge of the narcissist's tool kit, we can recognise 'withholding' for what it is and not confuse it with shyness or social anxiety.*

# Chapter 8 - Disassociation

One evening, The Mother, my younger sister and I encountered a mugging whilst walking through our local park. "He took my bag!" The echo was coming from far away. In response, The Mother picked up my younger sister and ran with her, away from the woman's screams. I fled, too, running as fast as I could. I stretched out my arm, trying to grasp her coat tail, flapping furiously in the wind. My legs were too small to keep pace. I fell behind quickly. Panic set in as she got further and further away.

For a time, there was nothing but blackness in front of me. Until I got close enough to see the swimming pool lights (from where she was collecting another sibling.) I caught a brief glimpse of her and noticed that she was continuing to run, full steam ahead. At no point did she turn around to look for me. She didn't put out her hand for me to grab or shout at me to run faster. It was as if she'd forgotten I was there.

I arrived at the pool, breathless, with my heart beating out of my chest. She was already there, mingling amongst the other parents, acting as if nothing had happened.

She didn't alert anyone that a mugging had just taken place, which confused me. My mind went to the lady. Why were we running away from her? Shouldn't we have helped her? And why are we now pretending that didn't just happen? She was crying out for help, and we ran in the other direction!

Even though we were now safe at the swimming pool, she still didn't acknowledge my presence, ask if I was OK, or allude to what had just happened. It felt like it was a dirty secret.

On the walk home, we saw the bruised and battered lady. She looked dishevelled and distraught. I was worried that she had no way of getting home without her purse. She asked The Mother if her face was still bleeding, to which she gave an unconcerned "no," without stopping to check, and carried on walking. Later that night, I told her that I was scared to go to sleep. She told me not to be so silly.

XXX

For years my mind had turned this mugger into a Big Foot bogeyman. A half man half beast, King Kong thing. It was only by doing trauma therapy that I uncovered that he was just a man. I also discovered through therapy that I'd buried the feelings attached to this memory. (Disassociation).

For the first time, I realised how guilty I felt for not helping the victim. But most importantly, I uncovered the pain that I'd done such an excellent job of suppressing all these years- the traumatic truth that she'd inadvertently exposed that night. A fact that even before this incident, I'd secretly feared.... that my existence was irrelevant to her.

That's what it feels like to be 'The Lost Child' – it's like you don't exist. I believe that all victims of narcissists disassociate to a degree to survive. The problem is, when it becomes a way of life, there's no way back to authenticity. This makes the building blocks of relationships, emotional intimacy, and trust almost impossible in later life.

*'**Disassociation**' - When we subconsciously bury feelings attached to a traumatic event (as a coping strategy).*

## Chapter 9 - Breadcrumbing

I never felt like The Mother knew who I was. She often made false accusations and blamed me for things I didn't do. So, it was confusing that she noticed my affinity with animals. One day, I came home from primary school to find that we had some ducks! Purely for my benefit! I don't know how long we had the ducks, but one day, shortly after, I came home…. the ducks were gone. Just like that! 'Where did the ducks go?' But I didn't feel it was OK to ask. The Mother never referred to them or their absence, so I felt she wanted me not to mention them either. So, I didn't. On a primal level, I felt scared that those that existed could disappear without even a mention. I've never asked her since what happened to those damn ducks!

Anyway, not long after this, she bought me a dog. A Yorkshire terrier. I immediately fell in love with her but had no idea how to take care of her. I relied on The Mother to teach me but I was too young to realise she had no clue either.

I noticed ticks on her back once, and I pointed them out, suggesting we use tweezers to pick them off. She looked at me disappointed and said, "I thought you liked animals!" I felt ashamed and confused. Of course, I wanted my dog to be healthy, but was I being abusive to the tics by wanting to remove them?! I have no idea whether she was that stupid or if she was being deliberately neglectful. Regardless, she was trying to convince me that I was cruel.

The fur on Yorkshire Terriers takes a lot of work, and it can quickly become matted if it's not brushed regularly. Of course,

I didn't know at the time that regular brushing would have avoided all the drama she went on to create. We ended up falling into a pattern of letting the dog become matted and then cutting the fur off. She aggressively approached the fur-cutting process and shouted and swore, which would trigger the dog, who'd growl aggressively back at her.

She'd put a sock over the dog's head to stop her from snapping and made me complicit in the abuse by demanding that I try to calm the dog down after she'd worked her up. Every time it was the same. She'd bark orders at me to "Take care of this fucking dog! She's your fucking dog! You say you care about her! Look at the state of her! Hold her down! Talk to her!" She was gaslighting me into believing I was entirely responsible for the dog's neglect, despite never having shown me how to look after her. (Gas lighting is creating an environment of confusion with the intention of distorting another's reality.) I feared her, so was too frightened to refuse her. And even if I hadn't been, I wouldn't have known what else to do.

My dog would squirm in an attempt to escape the whole ordeal, whimpering and growling and often getting cut in the process.

After many years of neglect, my dog was bald from untreated mange. Her teeth had fallen out, and she had cataracts in both eyes, making her almost entirely blind. Despite intuitively knowing that my dog wasn't being treated well, I wasn't conscious enough of these feelings to do anything about it.

My dog, Kerry, brought me lots of joy, and she was easy to love, unlike The Mother. I got a lot of warmth and affection from her, which made my complicity in her treatment all the more painful to bare.

XXX

So, why did these friendly gestures of getting the ducks and the dog go horribly wrong eventually? It was as if being nice was so uncomfortable for her that she somehow had to redress the balance. Creating the well-known 'hot and cold' technique. The purpose of which is to confuse. I eventually grew to distrust any 'kindness' from her for this very reason.

When people are subjected to breadcrumbing regularly, they tend to make these instances more than they are—believing that these are attempts at self-improvement. Unfortunately, the narcissist rarely does more than the bare minimum to keep us around.

*'**Breadcrumbing**' - Random acts of kindness. Another narcissist's tool for controlling their victims,' and maintaining their position of power. It's these rare moments of kindness that keep us enmeshed.*

# Chapter 10 – Trauma induced by others

I've already mentioned flying monkeys – those used by the narcissist to abuse or neglect by proxy. Below are examples of trauma induced by others who had no connection to The Mother.

I believe I attracted these people and situations into my life because I already identified as a victim. Bullies seemed to instinctively gravitate toward me for most of my life. It wasn't until I started to work on myself that my environment gradually began to change, reflecting my newfound sense of self-compassion and confidence. I rarely get bullied by others now, and if I do, they tend to leave my environment pretty quickly, because I no longer identify as a victim. However, this was a gradual process that took decades to change.

XXX

One day, whilst I was sitting silently in class, trying to be inconspicuous whilst all those around me applied themselves to the task at hand, I thought, 'I'm not pretty, and I'm not smart….. But I could be really good.'

I decided then that being 'good', especially good, was how I could please The Mother and gain her love. My perception of 'good' was, giving others what they wanted at all times. No exceptions. Never saying no – ever, even if it felt uncomfortable. In fact, the worse it made me feel, the better a person it must mean I am, I reasoned. I was to put aside my thoughts, feelings, and desires in the pursuit of The Mother's love.

I now know that this lack of boundaries is a common trait, both in abusers and in their victims. Neither of us knows where the line is. What's ok to say 'no' to, and what isn't. Unsurprisingly, this blurring of myself and others got me into uncomfortable situations.

I was very young, still in primary school, when I got a reputation for being 'easy' simply because I didn't know that I was allowed to say 'no'.

One particularly frightening encounter happened on a coach returning from school swimming lessons. I suddenly found myself surrounded by a group of boys who took turns forcibly kissing me—creating a circle around me so that I couldn't get out.

This incident didn't make me popular. Word got around quickly. Another girl in the class took it upon herself to take the moral high ground and give me an ultimatum to tell the teacher, what I was guilty of (in her mind), or she would. This kind of self-flagellating logic worked. I felt guilty and ashamed, so I assumed I was guilty. I volunteered a confession to the teacher in front of the whole class.

It never occurred to me to call this girl's bluff. It also never occurred to me that I was the victim in this situation. It never occurred to the teacher, either. She sent me to the headmistress, who said I was to sit in her room until I confessed that I "enjoyed it as much as the boys did."

'Well, I didn't, so I won't, and you can't keep me here forever', I thought.

So I silently sat in her office until The Mother arrived to collect me early. I'd been violated and frightened by a group of boys; threatened with exposure by a classmate; reported to the headmistress by my teacher; blackmailed by the headmistress to admit that I was a guilty party; and finally had all this shame and guilt reinforced by The Mother, who refused to speak to me on the way home.

All these traumas happened in the space of just a few hours. Of course, I couldn't process how unjust it was then. It was just another day, another reinforcement and confirmation that The Mother was right about me.

XXX

She only collected me from primary school every other day, thank goodness. She took turns with her friend who had a child at the same school.

One afternoon as her friend walked us home, I was attacked by a large teenager who stepped out of the oncoming crowd. The Mother's friend was so far ahead of me that she didn't see what had happened.

The girl pushed me with such force that I fell onto my back with my ankles flung over my head, exposing my knickers. I picked myself up and ran as fast as possible, away from the crowd's raucous laughter ringing in my ears.

When I caught up, she offered no words of comfort. I kept pace with her the rest of the way home, walking silently alongside her.

When I got home, surprisingly, The Mother seemed to notice something was off. She looked at me curiously and asked if I was ok, and I said 'yeah,' but never mentioned what had just happened.

It wasn't until the next day that her friend told her. The Mother asked me why I hadn't told her immediately. She seemed offended that I didn't look to her for comfort.

It seems that even though she couldn't provide me with emotional support, she wanted the 'supply' of me asking for it.

If she'd wanted me to know that I could have gone to her for comfort, this was her time to reassure me of that. But she didn't. Instead, she focused on how offended she was that she had to find out from her friend.

After the attack, The Mother still had her friend collect me every other day, and I still had to walk home the same way, past the same teenagers. And she only ever walked marginally slower than the day of the attack. I semi-jogged to keep up with her.

## XXX

My therapist helped me overcome this trauma with one Eye Movement Desensitisation and Reprogramming session. (EMDR). It's an approach that focuses on bringing our traumatised inner children out of the shadows. We reconnect with them through sessions conducted in a safe and protected environment, working on healing our traumatic memories using the brain's natural healing powers. We have space to feel (often for the first time) the pain of these memories. Eventually, we can reprocess the trauma, so it is no longer a trigger for us.

In hindsight, I now understand that all the times I've felt socially anxious, and all the times I've feared being exposed or humiliated in some way, have most likely been an emotional flashback to this moment.

I have no way of knowing if my siblings suffered a similar fate at the hands of others. Traumas outside of the home were rarely discussed.

***EMDR** - A trauma therapy often used to overcome PTSD (Post Traumatic Stress Disorder). It's generally not considered effective for CPTD. Please refer to 'Complex Post Traumatic Stress Disorder, (CPTSD)', for a more comprehensive explanation of CPTSD.*

# Chapter 11 - Narcissists are poor care takers

There was a defining moment in my childhood after which nothing I said was ever to be believed again.

I was playing 'Jacks' on the kitchen floor with a school friend. (This was how we entertained ourselves back in the day, before Xbox and the like came along!)

The Mother interrupted our game to ask, "Were you really unwell this morning?" (I'd said earlier in the day that I felt sick, so I did not go to school.) She asked if I'd said I was unwell because I wanted to spend the day with her. She looked down at me, smiling. A rare occurrence. I saw in her eyes a pleading, a wish for me to say, 'yes, I lied so that I could spend the day with you.' So, I gave her what I thought she wanted.

Her face fell immediately. I realised my mistake in seconds, but it was too late. She stepped over our game. "Well, now I know never to believe you again". And she didn't.

I wanted to say 'I'm sorry. I lied. I did feel sick.' But then I assessed that if I admitted to lying, just then, how could I prove that I was telling the truth this time? I couldn't. I thought it best to let her assume I was a liar rather than confirm I was one. I felt like I'd been tricked, and I had. She'd used my desperation to please her against me.

She didn't like attending to my needs. Now, she had the perfect excuse not to. If everything I said was a lie, she had no responsibility to take anything I said seriously. In that moment, she excused herself from ever responding appropriately, maternally, to anything I said, ever again.

It was only a short time after the 'Jacks' incident that I fell ill. I must have been about eight when she took my sisters and I to see a play. I'd been feeling unwell for days, so I didn't want to go. Regardless, I was forced to.

I was quiet and withdrawn on the bus, and she seemed to take this as an act of defiance or aggression and told my siblings to ignore my 'sulking;'. That I was 'just looking for attention'. So I sat alone, looking out the window, angry and hurt that nobody believed I was in pain.

Gradually throughout the evening, I started vomiting with diarrhoea. I couldn't focus on what was happening on stage. So I frequently went to the toilet. She growled at me to 'stop making a spectacle of yourself.' She said I was ruining the play for the audience and the actors and demanded that I stop making so many trips to the toilet.

I couldn't obey this order because I was becoming increasingly unwell. Between bouts of vomiting, I curled up quietly on my seat, and started to drift in and out of consciousness.

My final trip to the ladies ended with me coming too, whilst sitting on the toilet. I opened my eyes to see The Mother standing in the doorway with a concerned stranger. (I'd stopped bothering to shut the door by this point, as privacy was no longer a concern.)

Despite my semi-conscious state, I could hear the lady - "You need to take her to the hospital! She's sick!"

Only when someone saw that she was doing nothing to help me did she finally do something. When we got outside the theatre, I was dragged to the edge of the pavement. She, on one side, my sister on the other. Both held an arm each whilst trying to hail a taxi, even though she didn't have the fare. (She only ever took out the exact amount of money needed.)

She stopped a few taxis before one agreed to take us to

the hospital for free. My sister sat beside me in the back seat, slapping my face hard to keep me conscious. I wanted to push her hand away. The slaps hurt, but I didn't have the energy to raise my hand.

The taxi driver picked me up and carried me in to the hospital. I raised my head one last time to see blinding neon ceiling lights staring back at me; before finally, my head lunged back, and I fell into peaceful oblivion.

I felt safe and comforted in the arms of this stranger, whom I only remember was wearing a brown leather jacket.

It turns out I had appendicitis. As I lay on a gurney, with a nurse pulling my socks off, I was vaguely aware of The Mother. "She kept reaching and reaching and reaching". (She meant to say retching. The Mother has a funny way of mispronouncing words. No matter how often she's told, 'that's not the correct pronunciation', she continues regardless. Unaware of how silly this can make her seem to others. This embarrassed me sometimes, but at this moment, I was too disoriented to be embarrassed.)

I was left in the hospital overnight. I don't remember her saying goodbye. It's unlikely she did. I remember a moment of feeling scared before drifting off to sleep. I was aware of feeling abandoned, but the moment passed quickly. I was too sick to focus on anything for long, but just a moment before my eyes closed, I remember them filling with tears and feeling a lump in my throat.

XXX

It wasn't until years later that my sister shared with me that The Mother had lied to the doctor about my symptoms. She knew she'd ignored me for too long, so she rewrote the story, saying that I hadn't felt ill before leaving the house and that I suddenly got sick at the theatre only a short time ago.

During the two-week recovery period, she never once apologised for dragging me to that play when I was unwell or for delaying getting medical attention. (In hindsight, I'm grateful she did drag me to the play. Being in public is what got me the help I needed.)

A strange thing happened as a result of her withholding. As I recovered from the op at home, I convinced myself I hadn't had appendicitis. It was a pointless, exploratory operation because I was being so dramatic. Her lack of concern convinced me that I mustn't have been ill after all.

I don't know if she genuinely didn't believe me or if she pretended not to prolong my suffering. Either way, she appeared to be repelled by the extra vulnerability my sickness brought.

Vulnerability and/or sickness either disgusts or frightens her, I think, because a sick child demands a mother be a mother, to put the child first, to show empathy. This is something she just can't do. So, she withholds and becomes hostile instead.

XXX

Recently I requested my doctor's notes, and from there, I discovered that she eventually admitted to the doctor that I'd had a grumbling appendix for two days before taking me to the theatre. She was never challenged about this, and nothing in the notes suggests that they found her behaviour a cause for concern. This was one of the many 'missed opportunities' during my childhood.

I got the proper treatment because my older sister stepped in and told a doctor the truth. She recalls that he got angry and said to The Mother that if her withholding of information and delaying help resulted in consequences for my health, he'd hold her personally responsible. It wasn't often that others could see beneath the mask. She was rarely challenged like this.

*\*Narcissists are often poor caretakers. Partly because they don't like responsibility and partly due to their lack of empathy.\**

# Chapter 12 - Emotional Work

My natural state as a child was one of integrity and curiosity. I constantly sought connection and emotional intimacy, particularly with The Mother. I was desperate to prove my love to her and for her to recognise and respond to it. Sometimes the feeling of longing was all-encompassing, almost like a physical ache. Other times, it lay below the level of conscious awareness.

In desperation, I sometimes unintentionally challenged her with my need for truth and clarity. (This must have been quite repellent to someone whose whole MO is to disguise who they are!)

I was about eight when I precociously asked one hot summer's day, "Why do you love me?" We were sitting on the grass in the garden together. I suppose I seized the moment because there was a neutral stillness between us rather than awkwardness, which often made me withdraw and shut down. She didn't reply.

For a moment, we sat with the silence uncomfortably lingering between us.

I tried again. "I mean, I know why I love you. You feed me, you clothe me, you send me to school". (Repeating back to her one of her mantras.) "But why do you love me?..."

Crickets!

I imagine she hoped I'd move on if we sat in silence long enough. But I didn't. I could never forget that she was unwilling to say why she loved me. She didn't even attempt to respond. She just acted like she didn't hear me.

I could sense that she was shocked, but I didn't understand why. I'd seen enough TV shows to know that 'I love yous' were considered normal in many families. I wondered why she never said it, and it bothered me. As if the word 'love' was embarrassing or something.

Despite knowing that she didn't consider me pretty enough or clever enough to love, I still believed I could win her over if I just tried hard enough. I still believed that love lurked beneath her abrasive exterior. I was pushing to help her reveal this softer side of herself I was sure existed. I wanted to reassure her that it was ok to be vulnerable.

When I think back, I didn't feel loved, so I guess what I was asking was, 'Do you love me?' But this felt too confronting, so I asked in the way I did to hopefully gain some insight to help me understand what I needed to do to get her love.

My siblings opted out of trying to get The Mother's love early on. Unfortunately for me, I was slow on the uptake.

*Above is an example of the 'emotional work' I often did to establish intimacy with her. Little did I know - narcissists avoid emotional intimacy. They find it, at best, uncomfortable. At worst, repugnant. They fear emotional intimacy because they've cultivated a false self to get through life. Emotional intimacy risks the false self-being exposed.*

# Chapter 13 - Another frame of reference

For the most part, The Mother ensured I had only one frame of reference – her. But there were brief moments that provided me with a different perspective. She couldn't control the behaviour of other adults all of the time, no matter how much she may have wanted to.

I barely knew her friend that visited one day. Despite this, I instinctively gravitated towards her. On one visit, I ended up with my arms and legs wrapped around her, as she rocked me back and forth like a baby. I was too old to be cradled this way, but she readily gave me the affection I didn't even know I'd been craving my whole life.

As I was enjoying the sensation of being rocked, I heard The Mother say "I've never hugged her like that. I suppose I should do that". But she never did.

I believe this moment of connection, and the connection I seemingly had with my dad long ago, somehow anchored me. These brief feelings of connection allowed me to believe in love, and I needed this belief to survive my childhood.

Despite her inability to show me love, affection or compassion, there were many times when The Mother looked to me for compassion and sympathy.

She told me once how she found my Nan to be cold. I have no way of knowing if there was any shred of truth in this. However, my tiny amount of time with my Nan was positive. She was warm to me. She didn't hug me or kiss me, but I was comfortable enough with her to sit on her lap.

My only two memories of her are her teaching me the 'Our Father' (The Lord's Prayer) and then her crying when it was time for us to leave Ireland to return home.

XXX

I don't remember why my Nan and I were alone the evening she taught me the 'Our Father'. I do remember that we sat together beside the range, nice and toasty. Cosy. A contrast to life in The Mother's house, which was always cold, even in summer.

That night, she discovered that I didn't know the prayer by heart and was horrified. She lifted me onto her knee and showed me how to clasp my hands together in prayer. She proceeded to teach me, line by line, through patient repetition. I learned the whole prayer that night.

Others perceived me, (The Mother, teachers, etc.), to be a slow learner, but I took to learning in this warm and patient environment easily.

The one to one attention, and her willingness to teach me, had always been a private memory I'd never shared with anyone until now.

The last time I saw her alive, the day we left Ireland, she cried a lot. I felt terrible about leaving her. She gave me 50p as we left the house for the last time. I tried to assuage my guilt by returning the 50p.

XXX

Maybe she was how The Mother said she was to her, but to me, she was nice. It's impossible to tell whether The Mother was running a smear campaign against her mother, or, my Nan was being duplicitous by being warm towards me, having never been able to be that warm towards her. Who knows?! I could drive myself crazy thinking about these things. All I know is my Nan was one of the few adults in my life who didn't seem to buy into The Mother's narrative about me. She was kinder to me than all my uncles and aunt.

## XXX

The Mother somehow managed to create no other frame of reference even though there were three other people in the house, all with access to the outside world.

If there were the emotional freedom to communicate honestly with each other, we would all have been privy to each other's take on things, but none of us were, because The Mother had somehow made honesty a crime.

We witnessed cruelty to the other, lies and gaslighting of each other; but none of us ever spoke up. None of us united against her.

*Narcissists tend to isolate their victims in a pre-emptive strike by being their only frame of reference. One of the ways they do this is by running a 'smear campaign' against their victim. So, if they ever wake up to the abuse, they will have no one to tell and nowhere to run to.*

# Chapter 14 - Coercive Control

The Mother became more controlling in my teens. However, I was first aware of her excessive need for control just before puberty.

On one holiday, at a Butlin's site, when I was about 10, I made the mistake of agreeing for her to hire a pedal go-kart for us.

The sun was shining as we walked along the site, holding hands. She seemed in a good mood. Ordinarily, she was a taskmaster, always pushing me to do better and be better. But on this day, she seemed relaxed. (Breadcrumbing lowers the defences of the victim.)

She hired a go-kart and used it first. At the time, it didn't strike me how odd this was that she, the grown-up, insisted on playing with the toy first. Only passing it to me, the child once she'd tired of it.

I felt happy and thought we were connecting, bonding, and doing something together. After peddling around the site for a while, I returned to our chalet, tired and thirsty. She looked puzzled when she saw me. "What are you doing back here?" I got out of the go-kart. She looked offended. "I can't believe you made me rent that for you. What a waste of money!"

I didn't want to offend, even though I was tired and bored of it by now. "I'm not done. I just stopped to get a drink."

"Well, hurry up. Get back on it. You need to get your value for money!"

I begrudgingly peddled around the site again. On my return, she sat in front of the chalet as if on watch, ensuring I didn't stop.

"Go on! Keep going! Keep going!" Around the site, I went again. I had to peddle that thing for nearly four bloody hours! Talk about taking the fun out of something!

That last time she was sitting outside the chalet, there was amusement in her eyes. I could see that she enjoyed the control. I also understood that she enjoyed that her feelings mattered enough to me that I was willing to put myself through discomfort so that I didn't disappoint or offend her.

Coercive control is subtle, so it's only tried on those that allow it. I never witnessed The Mother coercively control my siblings, so I believe that both she and I felt that because they wouldn't allow it, I had no choice but to.

*Narcissists are often 'killjoys' and will ruin special events, making them difficult to holiday with. Their envy is so pervasive that it extends to not wanting others to have fun.*

## Chapter 15 - Narcissists don't grieve like others

Dad died when I was 10. The Mother was told of his death in front of me. Neither adult acknowledged my presence. Both acted as if I didn't understand what they were saying.

On the day of his memorial, she didn't tell me what was about to happen. I picked up on things just by listening and observing.

On leaving the church at the end of the service, I got tearful. Overwhelmed by the number of people that came to say goodbye to him. There was an overspill outside of nearly a hundred people.

An older cousin put her arm around me as we walked outside. She must have only been about 15, but she was the only person who seemed to notice I was upset. And the only person that tried to comfort me.

The Mother rolled her eyes as if I was a drama queen and spat out, derisively, "Sure, she (meaning me) doesn't understand."

My cousin fired back protectively, "Yes, she does!"

This was one of the few times I saw someone stand up to her … and she didn't clap back. She just responded with an inane grin. Her lack of compassion made my tears dry up immediately. I saw no point in looking for comfort from her.

xxx

My Nan died a few months later. The Mother placed us all with various people so she could return to Ireland for the funeral. I had a best friend; but instead, she placed me with relatives I barely knew.

For the first time in my life, I started to look forward to school whilst I was living with relatives, because it was the only way I could catch a glimpse of my younger sister in the playground during break. I missed her desperately.

I had two coping strategies that got me through this unbearably lonely time. I kept myself as invisible as possible and dreamt up a fantasy 'Brady Bunch' life in my head. One kept me safe, whilst the other kept me from dying of boredom.

The Mother didn't contact me once while I was with relatives. And when she returned, she never asked anything about my stay. She still didn't even explain why she'd gone to Ireland. I had to find out from a school dinner lady.

Later that day, on the way home from school, I asked The Mother, "Is Nan dead?" She continued walking with a fixed gaze, looking ahead. There wasn't a flicker of a response in her eyes or her face. She simply said "Yes". And that was the end of the conversation. I wonder how long she would have left things unsaid. Or if she ever would have told me that my Nan had died!

XXX

I had no idea how my siblings felt about these losses. They weren't discussed. My younger sister was too young to process such things, I think. Whilst my older sister was too busy being a teenager, and my brother was too busy being angry at the world. So, none of us ever shared our grief. It was as if we lived within a simulation where feelings didn't exist.

*Narcissists withhold information because it is a form of currency (i.e. power) to them.*

## Chapter 16 - Crocodile tears

As a last resort, narcissists will go pathetic, especially when they feel that outright aggression or passive aggression isn't an option. (Passive aggression can be just as intimidating as overt aggression and even more psychologically damaging because there's a layer of confusion added. The narcissist often takes advantage of our confusion and uses gas lighting to avoid accountability for their behaviour.)

They can often turn tears on for other people at the drop of a hat, which may be why it's so hard for their victims to find support. They do a good job convincing everyone, including their victim that it is, in fact, they who are the victim. Here's an example of just that.

For years, The Mother had threatened to put me into care. I suspect she didn't because it would've damaged her self-sacrificing image, especially as I wasn't a difficult child.

After years of being repeatedly told to 'fuck off out of here when you're 16'; 'you're an embarrassment and a disappointment'; 'I regret the day that you were born'; 'if I'd known you would have turned out like this, I would have had an abortion'; 'I wish I had never had you'; after years of being brainwashed by all these mantras, I decided to run away with a school friend, at the age of 11.

It seemed like a logical solution that I thought she'd be happy about. I was doing her dirty work, after all. Abandoning myself so she didn't have to.

My friend and I had planned it for a while. We even discussed it with the school counsellor, who chuckled and said it would be best to wait till summer.

We agreed to run away at the end of the school day. We had no idea where we were going or what we'd do. We just knew we weren't going home.

With such little preparation, the plan only took a few hours to disintegrate. By dinner time, we were cold and hungry. Suddenly I started to wonder what she would be feeling. Would she be worried? Angry? I began to feel fearful of her possible reaction. Then the guilt set in.

We walked into a police station and told them we were runaways, and without much probing, the police drove us home. I cried in the back of the car, regretting the shame I was about to bring her.

When she opened the front door, she was crying. I was shocked, and immediately remorseful. I took her tears to mean that she'd been worried about me. For a split second, I thought I'd made a colossal mistake. 'She wasn't happy I ran away! She was sad! She does care about me!'

The police left. She turned on her heels without a word and walked towards the kitchen, where she silently started to prepare me some eggs and chips. I followed her, expecting some kind of interaction.

I looked on, quietly, unsure of myself and hesitant, as she prepared dinner. I noticed that her eyes had dried, and her face had hardened. She refused to look at me or talk to me.

It dawned on me then that I'd been right all along. She didn't care about me. I retreated from her passive-aggressive silence and gravitated towards the lounge, where I attempted to absorb myself in the distraction of the TV. I went to bed later that night, knowing that she'd probably never forgive me for what I'd done. We both knew she didn't want me; that was a given. Now I knew I couldn't let anybody else know. It was our secret.

In trying to free her from a responsibility she didn't want, I'd inadvertently exposed her. She didn't want me to run. Despite frequently telling me she couldn't wait to be rid of me. She wanted me to stay and endure the suffering. She wanted me in this double bind she'd created for me because to be in a double bind is to be paralysed and weakened.

XXX

Tears were not something that was accepted within our family as a normal expression of pain. Unless the tears fell down The Mother's cheeks, of course. On the rare occasion, tears fell; they did so silently onto a pillow in the darkness of night. The holding back of tears led to a painful lump in the throat as if razor blades had been swallowed. And still, the tears fell silently so as not to be accused of looking for attention.

*Narcissists feel a more narrow range of emotions than most people, and the emotions they feel are often shallow, so they can change quickly.*

# Chapter 17 - Guilt

She only ever brought up my running away once, several months later. I'd been locked out of the house one rainy day. (This was a fairly common occurrence. She didn't consider me mature enough or trustworthy enough to have a key. So I'd have to wait for my younger sister, who was in primary school, to arrive with her key.)

On this particular day, the rain was coming down in sheets. With no shelter or sign of her or my younger sister, I made my way to my uncle's house 10 minutes down the road.

I phoned home every 10 minutes, anxious not to worry her. An hour passed. She eventually picked up the phone. Just as I was about to explain myself, she aimed and fired, "Up to our old tricks again, are we?" I felt as if I'd been punched in the stomach. It seems she was waiting for the right moment to throw back in my face the (limited) distress I'd caused her by running away.

Now, as an adult, I believe she was faking being hurt in that moment. Just like I believe she faked tears the night the police dropped me off.

A large part of her power and control over me was her ability to manipulate me into feeling guilty. So, often throughout my life, I've felt that stinging pain of the metaphorical sucker punch. The same pain I felt that day. I was so overcome with guilt and shame that I couldn't think clearly.

However, with hindsight, since the fog has cleared, I can process that it was well over an hour since I was due back from school. Yet, she made no attempts to look for me. My uncle's house would have been the most logical place to look, as he was the nearest relative to us geographically, and we frequently popped in on him. That would have been a logical conclusion, considering the torrential downpour we'd just had. Yet, when she got home, she didn't ring him to see if I was there. She did nothing.

So, I don't believe she was at all concerned. But she was able to spin things around like lightning. She was able to make me feel guilty for sheltering from the rain! I returned home to a punishing frosty silence. She never did allow me to explain myself.

I now understand this technique of the narcissist is called 'controlling the narrative'. If I'd been allowed to speak, it would have become apparent quickly that there was no reason to be angry with me. After this incident, I reflected that the only other option I had was to sit in the rain and wait for her.

If she'd returned home to see me sitting by the front door like a drowned rat, no doubt she would've told me that I was stupid not to shelter at my uncles. 'A simpleton', she used to call me.

The double bind, again. A few years later, I did choose to sit out in the rain rather than shelter at my uncle's house. But she didn't get to chastise me. A kindly neighbour saw me out of her window, invited me into her home, and gave me tea and biscuits while I waited for her return.

Guilt tripping is another form of gaslighting. It's designed to make the victim believe they're an awful person and so deserve their mistreatment.

*Narcissistic parents sometimes pretend to be angry or hurt because they know that a loving parent would feel this way in that circumstance. They mimic the emotions they think should be displayed, which can sometimes be confusing and contradictory because it's not genuine.*

# Chapter 18 – Narcissists isolate their victims

The Mother learned with my older sister that sending her to the local comprehensive provided her with another frame of reference, which inevitably weakened the control The Mother had over her. She was not to make the same mistake with me. I only attended the local comp for about a year before she told me it wasn't good enough. Narcissists are opportunistic and know how to take advantage of a situation and make it work.

It was true that it wasn't a good school. There were discipline issues, and the results were poor. However, at 11, this wasn't a concern to me. I was just starting to come out of my shell, which I suspect, she wanted to nip in the bud. I believe that she feared me rebelling and so used the smokescreen of appearing to want to provide me with better education to remove me from my support network.

Just as I was starting to become more confident, I lost it all by having to become the new girl. During the entrance interview with the headmistress, The Mother asked for me to be put back a year. In front of me, she told the headmistress that I wasn't very bright, and she didn't think I could manage in my chronological year. The headmistress readily agreed, without even looking at me. So right there, a whole year of my life just vanished.

The hypocrisy and irony are not lost on me now (although it was at the time.) The Mother was forcing me to endure the same humiliation she'd experienced at school. (She was made to repeat what we'd now call Year 6; and was required to repeat it again. Until her parents gave up on her, took her out of school, and enslaved her on the farm.)

XXX

Now, I was utterly alone. I was in a different school from my sister, and an hour and a half away from my home and local friends. The longer journey put extra pressure on me, eventually causing me to drop out of swimming (an activity I'd enjoyed for the last four years.) Over time I stopped seeing my local friends too.

For the first year in my new school, I was completely ostracised by my classmates. The only reason I could think of for this horrible treatment was that I was new and had a different accent. I lived in a working-class area, and the school was a wealthy one.

No matter how nice I tried to be to others, I just didn't fit in. I ate lunch alone for a whole year, sometimes in the toilet, so I didn't feel so conspicuous.

After a year, girls from another class allowed me into their friendship group, so lunchtimes got easier, but it was yet another year before my classmates would accept me into their friendship group.

Once I tried to tell The Mother how unhappy and lonely, I was, she just told me that I didn't need friends.

My confidence never recovered from this move, and I quickly became more introverted and self-conscious.

When I agreed to change schools to improve my academic chances, it didn't occur to me that my peers would hate me so much. Until then, despite adults not liking me, I was always popular amongst my peers.

*Narcissists are a walking contradiction in a lot of ways. They hate us, their victim, because they need us. They are irritated by our presence. Yet, at the same time, they feel compelled to isolate us from others, thereby keeping us closer. (I had no social life, because I had no friends, so I was at home all the time now, outside of school hours.)*

# Chapter 19 - Narcissists are horrible gift-givers, unless they're 'love bombing'

Like most narcissists, The Mother is mean. She seemed proud of this in private, despite acting generous in public. Her hatred towards me dramatically increased the year my older sister left home. It seemed that this gave her a new freedom to express her hostility more openly.

I was nearly 12 when she told me I would never receive another birthday or Christmas present again. I'd not shown enough gratitude for my presents the previous year apparently. (Narcissists hold grudges and play the long game.) She rationalised her withholding of gifts by blaming me.

XXX

It was the Christmas before my 11th birthday. She'd bought my younger sister and me the same novelty Mickey Mouse reversible jumper. She also bought me 'The Complete Works of William Shakespeare'. (I forget what else she bought my sister.) I dutifully wore the hideous jumper at least twice and pretended to be enthralled by the boring Shakespeare book.

I was just getting into hair and make-up and enjoyed music. So, cartoon characters and heavy exam reading material way beyond my years were not things I displayed any interest in, funnily enough! She completely ignored who I was, and bought presents for the child she wished I was. Someone more intelligent, yet more immature than myself. An interesting juxtaposition! An immature genius with poor fashion sense.

I was struck by the dichotomy of these presents even then. As if they were bought for two different people. I was embarrassed by the Mickey Mouse jumper, and the book made me feel inadequate. On receiving the gifts, however, I smiled and said thank you politely, trying to navigate the treacherous waters of her delicate sensibilities.

I didn't react authentically because I'd already learned it wasn't worth the fallout. I was always hyper-vigilant around her reaction to gift giving, often exaggerating my gratitude. This Christmas, I didn't do that because I didn't like how the presents made me feel. I was punished for not performing like a seal for the next 11 years.

Every Christmas and birthday after this, she'd remind me why I wasn't getting a present, pre-emptively and aggressively. As if she was expecting an argument from me (which she never got.)

Of course, it's always possible that she was just a terrible gift-giver with no malice. But knowing her the way I do, I believe that she deliberately gave me presents I wouldn't want, to then present me with the excuse for her withholding of gifts. (Problem-Reaction-Solution – a trick politician's use.) She created the problem (by buying me inappropriate gifts). She used my predictable reaction (not being particularly grateful) to justify her solution to the problem – (not to bother buying me gifts anymore.)

Although petty, this is a typical narcissistic move and requires some mental gymnastics to figure out.

I never discussed with my younger sister how she felt about our matching Micky Mouse reversible jumpers. I trust she didn't like them much either, as I never saw her wear hers.

*Narcissists often use gifts, money, and special occasions to control and punish their victims.*

# Chapter 20 - The Silent Treatment

As painful as withholding is, the silent treatment is more deadly. It's more passive-aggressive, and therefore, harder for victims to ignore.

The first summer my older sister left home, The Mother decided that we (her, my younger sister and I) would holiday in Blackpool. I could never have imagined that holidaying with her could be worse than being dumped on relatives that didn't know me. I was wrong.

She ruined the holiday by not speaking to me for the first three days, and I never even knew why. Not long after we arrived, I'd done or said something to offend her.

(It's awful enough to be subjected to the silent treatment when we have other distractions around us, like school and work, but on holiday, there was no escaping her cruelty.)

Initially, I coped with denial, hoping that if I acted as if things were ok, they'd eventually be ok. This made no difference. Then, I thought that giving her some space may help, so I retreated into myself. That didn't help, either. As a last resort, I fawned over her, and bought a cup in a souvenir shop that said something like 'best mother in the world'. She burst out crying and put her arms around me. I cried and hugged her back thinking 'Hurray! I've fixed it'. Relief briefly washed over me.

I was still distraught that she hadn't said anything to me for days, and I wanted to know what I'd done. But I also knew that bringing it up could make her angry again, so I gratefully accepted her crumb, of acceptance or forgiveness, whatever it was, and tried to move on from it.

There was a period of respite, during which I looked forward to enjoying the rest of the holiday. However, hours later, she became silent again. I eventually gave up trying to solve the mystery and so gave up trying to make amends. I just retreated further into myself whilst holidaying in hell.

XXX

I've come to believe that I didn't do or say anything to upset her. I believe she gave me the silent treatment for no reason other than it put her in a position of power. Her behaviour had me feeling guilty, and ashamed for no reason. So, in my efforts to appease, I fawned over her. It was the best I could do, as I never saw how to resolve conflict amicably and respectfully.

*The silent treatment is a powerful tool that can make victims believe they deserve their treatment. Once the victim believes this, they will allow the abuse to continue because they will not perceive it as abuse.*

# Chapter 21 – The narcissist's victim persona

After being shamed at four years old for expecting a hug from The Mother in the street, I knew not to be demonstrative in public. This never seemed to be an issue for her until years later, as I was leaving for a school trip. Suddenly, she moved the goalposts without warning. Acting offended that I did exactly as she'd taught me to do all those years ago, in that soul-destroying moment when I rushed up to her excitedly with my arms outstretched.

My classmates and I, together with our parents, gathered at the school gates early that morning. There was an excited buzz surrounding the morning mist. Eventually, after some awkward hanging around, we were advised that it was time to get on the coach.

I hovered for a while, wanting to hug and kiss her goodbye, but I was scared to. In case she would reject me publicly. She stood stiff as a board, refusing to initiate the goodbye or make eye contact.

Eventually, I had no choice. It was time to go. As I turned around to leave I heard her say sorrowfully to my friend's mum, "She's never done that before. I feel quite upset. She didn't even hug me. Great goodbye!"

I felt rooted to the spot, frozen in time, as I stood with my back to her. Scared to turn around to face her, but too guilt-ridden to move on. I didn't have the strength or maturity to confront the issue. But I knew I felt mortified. A wave of self-hatred washed over me. I'd done the wrong thing AGAIN! 'When will I ever learn?!' I thought.

Throughout the trip, my mind was plagued almost continuously with guilt, shame and confusion. This time I made no attempts to make things better with her. Instead, I silently stewed in my self-flagellating ruminations. Another holiday ruined.

XXX

In this respect, I didn't feel different from my siblings. I never saw her show any of them affection. But unlike them (seemingly), it was something I craved from her and relentlessly pursued well into adulthood. Whilst they, much more intelligently, gave up on her long ago.

*Narcissists are rigid by nature, but hypocritically, they frequently change the rules for us. If we're in a state of confusion, we're easier to control.*

# Chapter 22 - Narcissists have superficial relationships

For most of my childhood The Mother was single. Defiantly so. She never displayed any interest in having a romantic relationship. Quite the opposite. She was vitriolic towards men.

Some of her favourite mantras were 'Men are bastards' and 'men never grow up.' She seemingly decided that the reason my dad left her, and the reason her dad was an evil psychopath was simply that they were male. Therefore, she seemed to think all men were to blame for her suffering. She displayed her man-hating hostility as if it was something to be proud of. As if she were above such things as romance and intimacy. She acted nun-like, prudish, embarrassed, shocked. Even disgusted, by any discussion around sex or relationships. This changed suddenly. She started dating casually when I was about 11. Not surprisingly, no one lasted very long.

As young as I was, I noticed that all her date nights consisted of the date paying for dinner. There seemed to be a superficiality to these interactions that made me uncomfortable. I saw that she was out for what she could get. Her approach to relationships repelled me. So I looked to TV and books for guidance instead.

When I was about 12, I witnessed her have her first serious long-term relationship since my dad. The beginning of this relationship was somewhat traumatic and very confusing for me.

There was no introduction to her new boyfriend. There wasn't even an explanation that he was, in fact, her boyfriend. One evening he came to collect her for a night out as several men had done before, and the following day he was in her bed!

This was so incomprehensible to me at first that when I woke to see his car in the driveway, I thought there must have been some problem with his car! I assumed that he was sleeping in the lounge out of necessity. So, I tiptoed into the kitchen and made myself breakfast quietly to avoid waking him. Out of respect for his privacy, I ate my toast quietly in the kitchen, alone.

After a good hour or so of silence, I got curious, I suppose, and kind of frustrated. It must have been nearly midday by this point. I peeped my head into the lounge to discover it was empty. Amidst the shock and confusion I felt, I also registered, for the first time, a realisation of her hypocrisy. She wasn't who I thought she was.

It was impossible to reconcile this new behaviour with who she'd presented herself to be my entire life, even up to the night before.

I did the only thing I could when they finally got up. I acted as if I wasn't fazed or confused. I felt a responsibility to act as if this was normal.

XXX

I never saw anyone influence her the way this boyfriend did. Of course, I'd seen her flakiness. If someone well-educated or well-spoken enough liked a hobby, she would take it up, too. But I never saw her humble herself in front of another the way I saw her do so with him.

XXX

Very recently, I've started to wonder if he was also a narcissist. He knew that she liked the 'stuff' rather than intimacy. And didn't mind delivering it in abundance.

He arrived every Friday night with a week's worth of shopping and then chauffeured her to dance the night away. (He was tee-total. Something she'd specifically asked for in her lonely-hearts ad). He paid for the entrance fee and the drinks all night. She got to be on the arm of a wealthy man who was funny, confident and amiable. Then she got chauffeured home by him in his big expensive car.

The night hadn't cost her a penny. And all she had to do, for this positive narcissistic supply was weekly sex, followed by a heart attack breakfast the next morning. (Which did eventually induce a heart attack. And diabetes, too).

Not really. I'm not suggesting she can claim full responsibility for his health issues. He was grossly
overweight when they met; however, she did enable his poor eating habits.

XXX

Despite not being good caretakers, narcissists like to enable dependency in others to ensure they don't leave.

*Narcissists become the person they think they need to be to get their needs met. So, they're different things to different people. Because they need different things from different people.*

# Chapter 23 – Puberty threatens the narcissist

The following defect The Mother focussed on after my supposed lack of intelligence, plain looks and shyness was my weight, and the size and shape of my hips, in particular.

Her obsession with my body coincided with puberty, but it seems she was obsessed with both. From what I could tell, she didn't seem to have the same obsession with my sister's bodies, although she was equally neglectful when meeting their needs as pubescent girls.

Her disdain was reserved for my body alone. Her fixation consisted of paradoxical and simultaneous neglect and obsession. An obsession that combined fascination and disgust in equal measure. I now believe her obsession to be based on a mixture of envy and rage disguised as disgust.

The narcissistic parent is envious of their child's youth, innocence, future, and the possibilities that lay before them. My weight became a focal point on which to channel her rage.

She was demonstrably shocked and embarrassed by my changing body. As if it had never occurred to her that I would grow up one day! I believe her disdain towards me was partly because my body shape didn't reflect hers. My dad's DNA showed up in my body, face, and character traits, not hers. So, being reminded of the man who left her was more than she could bear.

She would relieve herself of her pain by frequently shouting the mantra, 'You're just like your father. Absolutely fucking useless!' (I never really knew what she meant by this because she'd refused to tell me anything about him, even when I asked.)

I believe she was envious of my bourgeoning sexuality and what it represented – Independence, and someone else eventually becoming more important than her.

My shame at my body not being what she wanted it to be intensified as she neglected to buy me appropriate clothing for my changing body.

'Was she so horrified and disgusted that she couldn't bear to look?' I wondered. 'Was that why I didn't have any clothes to fit me? Or did I not have clothes to fit me because I was monstrously and disgustingly overweight? Was it my fault? After all if I'd stayed the same size, I wouldn't need new clothes, would I?'

I had no bra months after I needed one. When I could no longer cope without, I looked for and found some old bras my older sister had left behind. Along with other items of clothing she'd decided not to take with her. I had no choice but to wear her bras, even though they were ill-fitting and uncomfortable. (My shape was bigger than hers.) This further intensified my shame. Eventually, when I couldn't fit into my older sister's hand-me-downs anymore, I resorted to wearing my school PE kit at home.

XXX

Remembering how I eventually got my first bra is particularly cringe-worthy. One day The Mother returned home from shopping with my aunt, who was visiting us, from Ireland, at the time.

She threw a brown paper bag at me, scoffing that she had got me a 'present'. For a moment, I was pleased. I thought she was being kind and thoughtful. Imagining it was a cake from a bakery or something. I was too innocent to notice that she was setting me up for ridicule. Only when I opened the brown paper bag did I realise why she was giggling like a schoolgirl. After seeing the bra, I looked at her in confusion. We'd never had a conversation about my needing a bra.

She retreated to the corner of the room, with her hands covering her sniggers. My aunt stood in the other corner, silently watching, seemingly bewildered.

I was more confused than embarrassed. However, I was embarrassed for her. She was acting as if she'd never seen a bra before! It was weird! I mumbled a 'thanks', then turned my back to continue my studies. It hurt my feelings that she found my changing body such a source of amusement.

It's clear now that I finally got my first bra because another adult, my aunt, told her I needed one. It embarrasses me to wonder how obvious this may have been to others. How long might I have had to wait if my aunt hadn't visited?

Later on, with my aunt no longer in sight, she insisted on me wearing the bra for her so that she could 'adjust the straps'. I didn't want her to do this. It was embarrassing. But saying 'No' to The Mother was never an option. I had no choice but to have her be up close and personal, whilst I stood there cold, semi-naked, and mortified. Aware that she was scrutinising every part of my exposed body.

This is an example of that confusing and contradictory behaviour I spoke of before. One minute, she didn't notice I needed a bra. (Seemingly). The next, she was intrusive. It didn't add up. This vacillation between ignoring my needs and overstepping my boundaries was typical and most apparent during puberty.

XXX

I started my period, having no idea what was happening, either. When I told her that I'd found blood and was concerned, she still couldn't bring herself to be the adult, even at that moment. Instead, she dumped the responsibility on my older sister, telling her to get me 'something' as she walked away.

I got handed a sanitary pad—something I'd never seen before. I had no idea what it was or how to use it. I figured it out with the 'common sense' she often told me I didn't have. Eventually, I suppose, from conversations at school, I figured out that I'd started my period. But that night, I went to bed wondering why I was wearing this nappy-like thing.

And so, the pattern continued. She was neglectful in providing me with essential things for my growing body but intrusive regarding things like shaving. At first, I was forbidden to shave. I obeyed this rule, until I saw that my younger sister had ignored it with no consequences. Her odd response to my sister's challenge was to ignore it, and instead demand the right to shave my underarms for me!

XXX

I believe she tried to make me feel so ashamed and embarrassed of my impending sexuality and changing body that my self-disgust and shame would create an ineptitude in my relationship skills (which it did.) If she could get me to hate my body, I'd be far less likely to want to share it with someone else.

In our adult years, my sisters shared their personal experiences of The Mothers' neglect and intrusion around their developing bodies too.

*Narcissists violate boundaries so consistently that the effort to keep them at bay can be exhausting. So, we frequently allow ourselves to be violated because it seems safer than incurring the terrifying wrath of the narcissist. In this way, they succeed in destroying our relationship with our self.*

## Chapter 24 - The narcissist needs their victim to think they're stupid

The Mother became increasingly obsessed with my academic achievement. Mine only. She had little to no interest in the academic achievement of my siblings. She'd convinced me I was getting this extra attention because I wasn't 'the full shilling'.

I'd assured myself that her overbearing interest in my education was her attempt at demonstrating love and concern. I perceived it as love, despite how toxic it felt.

One day, I came home to be greeted by her at the front door. "Don't take your coat off; you've got a French lesson." She sent me straight back out the door. I'd never expressed any interest in French, nor was I particularly good at it.

She often came up with random ideas like this. For me, only. I suspect that controlling the direction of my life gave her a thrill.

When I spoke to her about this as an adult, she denied this—telling me instead that I'd asked for these lessons because it was my dream to work and live in France one day! Of course, I knew this to be a lie. A defiant and condescending grin danced across her lips as she stared me out. As if to say, 'Go on! I dare you to challenge me.' I didn't.

She continued piling on the academic pressure unabated. I was only 12 when she enrolled me in an adult evening secretarial course. I have no idea what the typing school was thinking, expecting a 12-year-old to keep up in an adult class!

She never showed any interest in the results of my time and her money. She never cared what the outcome was. Only that I was busy. It's another form of control. Her thoughts were, I believe, that if I was busy doing, I wasn't busy thinking. It's a strategy cult's use.

One of the most traumatising experiences I was forced to endure under the guise of her 'interest' in my education was being sent on a French exchange alone for two weeks at 13 years old. The other English kids were all from a different school, so they all knew each other. I once again was the outcast—the only stranger amongst the group.

I repeatedly begged for weeks not to go but to no avail. She stonewalled all attempts at conversation. The night before my departure, I pleaded with her one last time not to make me go as she packed my bags silently.

Eventually, I had no choice but to accept my fate. The reality of what lay before me was terrifying. I hugged her from behind, trying to create some moments of comfort in my last hours before impending doom. She didn't respond to my hug.

I was sent to stay with a non-English speaking family (of course.) I felt so scared, depressed, and isolated the whole time I was there.

It's likely that for the first time, I had an awareness of how deliberately cruel she could be, probably because I could find no apparent rationale for her forcing me to live in a foreign country alone for two weeks. Especially given the fact that I was painfully shy and highly anxious. I knew she was aware of my shyness. She made it clear that she perceived it to be an embarrassing defect.

I couldn't convince myself that she was doing this for my benefit, no matter how hard I tried. The previous abandonments happened when I was too young to attempt to rationalise them. I didn't ask why she dumped us on her siblings in Ireland for 'holidays'. Or why she dumped me on cousins, I barely knew, when she went to Ireland for my Nan's funeral. When she could have placed me with my best friend or younger sister. I was too young to ask these questions at nine or ten. But at 13, I knew this abandonment wasn't for my good.

However, despite her cruel and neglectful intent, it could have been a positive experience if I'd exchanged with someone who was in any way communicative. Instead, I got someone who did not attempt to welcome me into her home.

Of course, I was used to being deprived of emotional intimacy, physical affection, and interesting conversation, but these two weeks felt akin to solitary confinement. I only had the English girls to chat with for a few hours daily, and I was often on the outskirts of those conversations because I was the outsider.

The Mother wrote once and rang once. I remember feeling tearful when I heard her voice. This didn't soften her.

On my return, she didn't ask a single question about my time in France.

The reversing of the exchange was also somewhat traumatic because of her predictable narcissistic attempt to undermine my feelings and distort reality. Siding with the enemy or others who abuse their victim is another favoured trick up the narcissists' sleeve. It doesn't matter who the person is or what the story is. The narcissistic parent frequently shows favourable treatment towards someone else's child. Particularly if this child and theirs' don't get along. The proverbial rubbing of salt into our wounds. It's bad enough to have a mother that doesn't like us. It's worse still that they seem to prefer someone else's child. But to prefer someone, who is horrible to us, is the worst.

I knew what she was doing because the French exchange girl had no redeeming features! She was dull, monosyllabic, and frankly rude. And yet The Mother gushed over her.

It wasn't until she started stealing from us right under her nose that she stopped sucking up to her. Eventually confronting the girl. Making her cry. But she still didn't apologise to me for trying to befriend a girl that made my time in France more traumatic than it needed to be.

The Mother would rarely own her feelings when challenged,

but I believe she paid for this trip because it gave her a two-week break from me. She abandoned me, albeit temporarily, under the guise of being a selfless mother providing her child with a 'fantastic educational opportunity.'

Privately, she made no pretence of it being an 'opportunity'. She didn't try to make me feel excited about the trip. And it was clear on my return that she had no interest in what I'd learned or experienced there.

XXX

There was never any jealousy from my younger sister regarding The Mother's obsession with my education. She never said, 'Why can't I do extra French lessons? Why can't I fuck off to France by myself for two weeks? Why can't I do a pointless secretarial course that I'll never use?' She seemed to know that The Mother's focus on my education was not for my benefit.

*Narcissists like to mould others into what they'd prefer them to be. But they don't understand that no matter how malleable their victim is or how successful they are in these efforts; it will never bring them joy. They will always be disappointed by their victim because their need to control, isolate and mould others comes from an inherent entitlement always to have what isn't theirs – their victim's soul.*

## Chapter 25 – The narcissist sees what they want to see

The Mother had an obsessive fear that I would be promiscuous from an early age, but, confusingly, she also completely ignored when men were being inappropriate with me.

After being forced to give up my swimming lessons, she decided that my sister and I could have a casual swim on a Friday evening so that she could join us in the pool. It was usually uneventful, except one time, when I went into the shower early because I had period pain and wanted to go home. It was a mixed-gender communal shower in which a male was already showering. I innocently showered beside him, closing my eyes, enjoying the warm water trickling down my body. (This was a pleasure I only enjoyed at swimming. We didn't have a shower at home and were limited to a once-a-week bath.)

I felt something touch my hip. I looked down and saw the man's arm outstretched. He was stroking me.

I panicked and ran out of the shower. My whole body was shaking as I frantically lunged into the pool. I rushed towards The Mother, fearing that my legs would give way.

When I got close enough, I cupped my hands around my mouth and whispered that a man had just touched me. I was on the verge of tears, and my voice was trembling with fear, but she didn't seem to notice.

"Tell the lifeguard", she said as she pushed off from the side, continuing her lengths. I didn't have time to process how uncaring her response was. I just did as I was told. Still shaking, with my heart beating out of my chest, I approached the lifeguard and told him. Immediately he got on his walkie-talkie, but they never found the guy.

As we left the pool, she didn't attempt to follow up with the staff about what had happened, demonstrating that what this man did, was of no concern to her. This is why I never shared with her what happened at gymnastics. I instinctively knew she wouldn't get it.

XXX

On a day trip to Littlehampton beach, her boyfriend molested me, right in front of her, underneath the water. He was looking at her as he did it. I thought I should tell her for a second, then I thought, 'no'. I had trouble believing what had just happened. I didn't know what to do except pretend it didn't happen. I moved away from him quietly and made sure to never be in such close proximity to him again.

After this, he started to talk provocatively to her in my presence. Comments that would have been red flags to most mothers. As time passed, he grew braver, his hints becoming less subtle. He indicated through his 'jokes' and comments that he was interested in pre/pubescent girls. He frequently pointed out the sizes and shapes of young girls. I watched this all go over her head.

XXX

By the time I'd hit puberty, I understood that I was not allowed to date through her avoidance of the topic. However, at least subliminally, it was also clear that this rule was based on her fear and shame of me dating, not any protective parenting philosophy.

Her watchful eye started to look for clues that I was engaging in sexual behaviour almost as soon as I'd started my period. I was about 13 when one evening she collected me from the local library, where I was studying with a boy. As we walked down the stairs out of the library, I looked up to wave goodbye. She tried to convince me that I'd given him a 'suggestive wink'. She then used this wink (that had never happened) as evidence of me being his girlfriend. When I protested that this wasn't true, she accused me of 'leading him on.' Saying I shouldn't have winked at him like that as it sends the wrong message! I couldn't convince her that there was no wink and no romantic relationship. He was just a dude I was studying with!

I suspect that she hoped she could reign me in with shame, by being accusatory. The best line of defence is attack, so they say.

*Narcissists are known to view their children as competition. As the child grows in confidence and maturity, the narcissist becomes more threatened. So, they will step up the gaslighting to stun and confuse their prey (child) into submission.*

# Chapter 26 - The narcissist lacks empathy

The next time I was horrendously ill after appendicitis, I was about 13. I'd been feeling sick for several days. Again, The Mother ignored my symptoms, insisting that she knew I was lying, and pretending to be sick for attention. So, I had no choice but to go to school, despite my constant nausea.

One day during break, I went to see the school nurse. Maybe it has something to do with being Irish, Catholic, or both, but she reacted precisely the same way The Mother would.

"Why is your mother insisting on sending you to school if you're sick?"

"I don't think she believes me. She thinks I'm pretending."

"What did you do to make her not believe you?"

"Nothing".

"There must be a reason she thinks you're lying. Do you lie a lot?"

"No".

"Then why doesn't she believe you?"

"I don't know."

I was sent out of sick bay and back to the classroom. A day or two after, I threw up at the bus stop on the way to school. The Mother always drove me to the bus stop, so she was there when I threw up. She went into a newsagent to get me some water. Then she told me to get on the bus. I was shocked that she still expected me to go to school. I said that I didn't think I could make it. "What if I'm sick again?"

She didn't respond. Instead, she returned to her car and left me to get the bus. I was stranded, nauseous, a 40-minute walk from home, and an hour and a half away from school, by bus.

I have no idea how I made it into school, but I wasn't in the classroom for very long before I started continuously vomiting. A friend was allowed to escort me to sickbay, where I spent the rest of the day.

The school nurse never acknowledged that I'd been telling the truth a few days ago. But her hostility transferred onto The Mother, whom she kept calling, to no avail.

At the end of the school day, my uncle came to get me. The same uncle that lived 10 minutes down the road. The nurse asked reception to request that he come to sick bay to collect me. When he arrived, she had no time for niceties. In a curt tone, she told him to relay a message to The Mother. That 'she should never have sent (me) to school knowing that (I) was unwell. It was irresponsible to be uncontactable when she knew the school would be trying to reach her'. She also instructed that The Mother take me to the hospital to get me checked out.

My uncle was gentle and patient with me in the car on the way home, driving carefully and slowly. He kindly pulled over frequently as the car's movement made me feel worse.

He was raised in the same house as The Mother, and at this moment, he demonstrated a level of kindness and compassion that she'd never been capable of. In the past, he'd made it clear that I wasn't his favourite, but at this moment, I was genuinely grateful that he was driving me home, not her.

She was in the driveway when we got to the house. She smirked as she saw my uncle get out of the car to approach her. She was pulling down the garage door as we pulled up, so I assume she'd just arrived home after having been out all day.

My uncle didn't relay the two first parts of the message. He seemed timid around her. He gently suggested that it was the advice of the school nurse that I be taken to the hospital. She scoffed at him in response. He left the scene, giving me a look that said, 'Sorry, there isn't more I can do to help.' I didn't get taken to the hospital.

Instead, she made me drink a cup of hot whiskey. Exhausted from all the retching, I curled up in a ball on a chair in the lounge. I must have dozed off. Soon, I was woken to the sound of aggressive banging on the back of my chair. She couldn't bring herself to shake me awake. That would involve touching me.

I already knew from when I had appendicitis that my being sick brought out the worst in her. "Wake up! Drink this!" She didn't explain what it was or why I should drink it. I didn't like it, but I followed orders. Her rage was bubbling on the surface now, so I knew just to do as I was told and don't ask questions.

The next day she told me that fish made me sick. She'd made a separate meal for herself and my sister and gave me left over fish. I don't think she'd planned to give me food poisoning. More likely, some old fish was lying around that she was too mean to throw out, so she gave it to me instead.

The morning I got sick at the bus stop, I believe she had plans and so wasn't going to let my sickness inconvenience her. Just like when I had appendicitis, she couldn't adjust to the situation at hand in the way we expect parents to be able to. She couldn't change her priorities because she only ever had one priority, and that was herself.

I think she was aggressive towards me once I returned home because she knew that the nurse knew what she'd done. I'd unwittingly exposed her again. Instead of feeling regret or shame and learning from the experience, she became enraged. It was my fault the nurse thought baldly of her.

*Narcissists react badly to their victim being sick for a multitude of reasons:*
*1. A lack of empathy. (They can't care, as it's not in their 'make-up' to do so.)*
*2. They don't feel responsible for anything or anyone – so a sick child is irritating to them unless they can get supply from the sickness.*
*3. They feel rage (and possibly envy) at the attention a sick person elicits. They secretly covet attention – constantly. So they loathe*

*to give that to someone else. We are there to serve their needs, to provide them with attention. Not the other way around.*

# Chapter 27 – The narcissist's obsession with physical appearance

I never thought about weight or food until The Mother started obsessing over it. I was slightly smaller than the average child and more active than most, and my fitness level was high with my twice-weekly swimming lessons and daily gymnastics. But then, one day, I woke up with hips, and suddenly nothing fitted anymore. Of course, that's not how it happened, but that's how it seemed.

It pains me now as an adult to think that if only my changing body had been accepted with compassion and maturity, if only I'd had new clothes, to accommodate my changing body, then I may not have gone on to develop a miserable obsession with my weight.

Instead, The Mother body shamed me frequently, particularly throughout my teens. A few incidents still cause a pang to the solar plexus when I think of them.

One day, while I was peeling potatoes standing beside her, she looked down at my legs and said, "Sure, I've had four children, and look at your legs compared to mine. They're enormous'" I carried on silently peeling potatoes, trying to swallow the lump in my throat.

Another morning I heard her talking on the phone to my private French tutor, who asked her if I would like to go swimming. The Mother told her I didn't want to go as I was on my period (which wasn't true). I overheard her say, "It would be good for her to go. It might help to shift that fat arse of hers. But I can't make her go."

I was so mortified that she was talking to my tutor about my body like this. The fact she'd lied didn't even register with me.

XXX

She also allowed others to talk negatively about my body to her in front of me. One sunny afternoon, we bumped into an elderly neighbour who stopped to chat with us. She commented that I'd gained weight, then reassured her, "don't worry. It's only puppy fat. She'll lose it soon enough." I never knew there was anything to worry about until she said, 'Don't worry.'

After years of failing at fad diets, I decided that the most effective plan would be to stop eating until I reached my goal weight 7st, (98lbs).

I expected some pushback from her, being as controlling as she was, but I was ready to stand my ground. I needn't have bothered psyching myself up because there was no pushback. She readily accepted my starvation diet (at only 14) with no discussion. After a day, she stopped bothering to dish up my plate. It wasn't until my older sister arrived home from her nursing training during the two-week Easter break that anyone acknowledged what I was doing. She immediately noticed I'd lost a stone after having not seen me in months. (14lbs). She told The Mother that it wasn't healthy for me to have lost so much so quickly.

My sister returned to her training, and The Mother continued to do nothing whilst I carried on starving myself. On our return to school, my younger sister confided in a teacher that she feared I might starve myself to death. So, the teacher pulled me aside. I was withdrawn and embarrassed, so refused to engage. Even though I had a nasty furry white tongue due to not drinking enough water, I was proud of myself. I wasn't ready to start eating again. I was scared that if I did, I'd never stop. I was so hungry! Every day was a battle not to eat. But I was winning.

Because of my reluctance to speak to my teacher, I suspect the school contacted The Mother. She never admitted this to me, but we were sitting in a psychiatrist's office days later, so I'm just putting two and two together.

By the time of the appointment, I hadn't eaten for 15 days. We saw two doctors, and at one point, we were separated. The older doctor spoke to The Mother 1-to-1 whilst I saw the younger doctor. I concluded early on that he was an idiot. I told him the truth. That I was an embarrassment and a disappointment. That if I were slimmer, maybe she would love me. "You need to say this to her when she comes in", he said.

'If I could speak to her honestly, we wouldn't be here, would we?!' I thought… 'Of course, I can't be honest with her! That's the whole point'! When The Mother and the older psychiatrist returned, he told me that he could tell from my breath that I was starving myself. (I had 'keto' breath because my body was burning fat so fast.) I felt embarrassed that my breath smelled but relieved that my body was burning fat. The Mother's ignoring of the situation had convinced me that I was still the same size, despite what the scales said.

XXX

On reading my doctor's notes, I discovered that I'd been diagnosed with 'depressive disorder, social phobia, a history of chronic low self-image, and anorexia'. He described me as a 'scared little girl, who is all too easily put down. Her concern about her shape is just one aspect of her poor self-esteem. She has difficulty expressing her feelings and comes over as a rather sad, lost girl. She's very undemonstrative and finds it difficult to express her anger.'

Only by reading my doctor's notes did I discover that his treatment plan was family therapy focused on helping The Mother to allow me more freedom. Family therapy never happened because she didn't attend the first two appointments.

I was then discharged without further investigation—another 'missed opportunity.'

*Narcissists are good at convincing professionals that they're loving, concerned parents. Because their abuse is primarily subtle in front of others, so it's often not picked up.*

# Chapter 28 - Fictitious Disorder Imposed On Another (FDIA)

The Mother didn't seem to get supply from me being genuinely ill. It just made her angry. However, it seems she got supply from making up that I was sick.

Her obsession with my health started manifesting when I was about 11 or 12. Gradually over the years, excessive appointments with specialists became the norm. However, I was dragged to these appointments whilst she ignored my basic needs. So I was too confused by this juxtaposition to understand what was happening. The doctors never figured it out, either.

'Her mother seems caring', one doctor noted. Yet, in the next paragraph, she quotes that The Mother refers to me as 'the black sheep of the family.' This doctor logged that she was pressuring me to stay in a school where I was so severely bullied that it made me clinically depressed. She seemed to think this was a good thing.

XXX

Doctors eventually came to believe that I had juvenile arthritis. So, I was referred to osteopathy. These appointments were always very embarrassing. I was required to strip down to my underwear whilst an osteopath; usually, a male, intrusively poked and prodded my semi-naked body. The worst part was feeling her eyes boring into me, scrutinising every inch, as I lay there embarrassed and helpless. She must have got bored of taking me to these appointments because, one day, they just stopped.

### XXX

Once I left home, the painful, itchy, swollen joints I'd suffered with all my life miraculously disappeared. I didn't have arthritis; I had chilblains! Which were immediately cured by living in a warmer environment.

Under her care, I wasn't allowed to ease my suffering with painkillers or anti-inflammatory drugs because 'there are risks and side effects with every drug.' She had the same excuse for withholding pain relief every month when I had painful periods.

### XXX

Why did she want to convince my doctors and I that I had arthritis? After doing some research, I'm convinced it had something to do with her wish to force molasses down my throat daily. I suppose she heard from somewhere that it had health benefits for bones. That may be, but it also contains high levels of sugar. She started to force me to drink a cup of molasses every morning shortly after that first psychiatrist's appointment.

Perhaps she was threatened by my losing weight. That may sound crazy, but it's also crazy to force a sugar-based drink on someone whose weight you're supposedly concerned about! How she forced this drink on me was evidence that it was not for my health. It was clear it was a power game.

The drink was vile and made me heave. I knew, though, from experience, that she was fickle, undisciplined, and easily tired of her own arbitrary rules. I knew that if I were initially compliant, she would start to loosen the reigns. Confident in the belief that she still had control of me.

I knew the game well. We'd been down this road many times before. At first, she was intimidating. I wasn't allowed out of her sight until the whole drink was gone.

Gradually, I was allowed to take the last few mouthfuls upstairs as I continued getting ready for school.

After several days of going unchallenged by her, I grew braver. I initiated, with no discussion, taking the full cup upstairs. After a few days of going unchallenged again, I contemplated throwing some of it down the sink. I stood on the upstairs landing, listening out for her. I could hear her pottering downstairs, but I couldn't hear her footsteps. She was far enough away for me to get to the bathroom sink unseen. My heart was pounding.

'What if she catches me' I thought, 'What will I say?...... Quick! Do it now, before she comes! If you keep dillydallying, she's going to catch you! Do it now!'

I tried to walk to the bathroom, cup in hand, casually. I turned on the tap first, so the remainder of the ugly thick dark concoction could disappear down the drain as quickly and quietly as possible.

I turned around. There was no one there. I walked back to my room, empty cup in hand. Mission accomplished! I did it! I felt triumphant, even though my heart was still pounding. Now that I'd succeeded once, I planned on pouring the whole cup down the sink every morning. And I did. Until one morning, she never gave me the cup of molasses.

This level of control over my diet was not unusual. For example, I wasn't allowed to become a vegetarian. I couldn't exercise this right until I left home. Other diet restrictions were placed on me frequently, such as not being allowed to drink tea.

I'm described as 'silently defiant' in my doctor's notes. I suppose I developed this nature by observing that she gave up power battles quickly if she could be fooled into thinking she was winning. I knew enough to bide my time, not to confront, to pretend I was doing as I was told, and then do as I damn well pleased.

To have any control over my life, I needed to be constantly on the ball, thinking ahead. She seized power again when I forgot this (usually due to daydreaming or brain fog). It was these times that she usually won.

XXX

It's known that there is a link between anorexia and controlling parents. Since coercive control is an element of narcissism, there is likely a link between narcissistic parents and anorexic offspring. However, I'm not aware of any studies around this.

*Statistics suggest there is no apparent link between 'Fictitious Disorder Imposed on Another (FDIA)' and Narcissism.*

# Chapter 29 - Narcissists are bullies

The same day her boyfriend molested me, I ended up with severe sunburn and painfully blistered lips simply because she wouldn't allow me to walk a few meters to get sunscreen and lip balm from his car.

As the sun beat down on my fair skin, I started to plead, "the car's right there!" within sight. She responded with her intimidating growl "to sit down and shut up." I was under such control that even though I could feel my lips and skin burn, I didn't dare move or complain again.

In the evening, I started to shiver badly back at his house. I was shivering and freezing cold, even though my skin was hot to the touch and red raw.

Because of her boyfriend's presence, perhaps, and her need to appear like a good mother in front of him, she treated my severe sunburn by rubbing calamine lotion all over my body. But not before forcing me to strip down to only my knickers.

I woke the next day with painful blisters covering my lips. For a week, I could barely eat or drink a thing. She never acknowledged that I was in such pain because she refused to allow me to walk to the car.

XXX

There is debate around whether narcissists are cruel deliberately or just unaware of others' needs due to their self-obsession. I guess it depends on where they are on the spectrum of Narcissism.

I believe The Mother to be a mid-range narcissist. There were moments I saw her trying to hide a smirk. Moments I knew she was getting a kick out of hurting me. Other times, like her not knowing where I was staying for gymnastics competitions, I believe was because it didn't occur to her to care.

*Narcissistic mothers view their daughters as extensions of themselves. Just like narcissistic fathers view their sons as extensions of themselves. We exist to reflect back to them a perfect version of themselves. But we must be careful not to do this too perfectly, or we could trigger their narcissistic rage.*

# Chapter 30 - Narcissists are envious

Back in the day, landlines were usually in the hallway. So, there was little privacy during a phone call. One evening I was chatting on the phone with a friend and laughed at something she said. At the end of the call, The Mother approached me. "I've never heard ye laugh like that."

Now, there are several ways to take this. She could have meant, 'it's lovely to hear you laugh like that.' But her facial expression and tone indicated that she was offended. So, it couldn't have been that.

It seems she was envious of my friend. There was even a hint of incredulity as if she was accusing me of fake laughing. Perhaps she was trying to self-soothe by imagining that my laughing was fake. This would mean I wasn't having as good a time as I was portraying. (Which would make her feel better.) This interaction left me feeling guilty for laughing with my friend and not being able to laugh with her.

XXX

One Saturday afternoon, I was invited to ice skating with a group of friends (both boys and girls). She couldn't object to this outing overtly because I wasn't breaking her rules. I'd be back to babysit before she went out in the evening.

However, this didn't stop her from feeling infuriated with me. She was bothered that I had plans and was going out to have fun. As the morning progressed, she became increasingly agitated and unreasonable.

Just before my friends knocked for me, she started roaming around the house, shouting at the top of her voice. (She did this often, walking around the house shouting to herself in rehearsed mantras about whatever pissed her off about me that day.)

Today it was my apparent obsession with sex. I suspect that the thought of me having male friends made her so uncomfortable that she had to sabotage it. When I heard the doorbell ring, I called out as breezily as I could, "My friends are here. Bye!"

As I opened the front door, my friends could hear her shout, "And keep your fucking legs together! I don't want ye coming home with no fucking baby!" There was a moment of stunned silence. None of us knew what to do. After a tumbleweed moment, I closed the door behind us. In silence, we walked down the street together for several minutes until someone, much to my relief, broke the tension with some random anecdote.

My friends never mentioned what they'd heard. They were as horrified as I was. However I never got invited to ice skating again.

XXX

The emotional deprivation at home forced me to find comfort in books. They gave me a reason to retreat to my bedroom. Fortunately, Judy Blume and Paula Danziger provided me with what felt like a safe space, even in that house.

I didn't process it at the time, but in hindsight, I could see that she was envious, even of my love of reading. She revealed this to me one evening as she was getting ready to go out.

I'd almost finished a whole book that Saturday. Only leaving my room to use the bathroom and to make myself snacks. So, we hadn't interacted much. She called me downstairs to put her necklace on. I descended the stairs with my head space still in my book.

As I was fiddling with her necklace, she exuded a silent hostility.

"What's the matter?" I asked.

"You've been in that bedroom all fecking day. You've not talked to me once!"

I was stunned that she looked like she was about to cry! I immediately felt intense guilt. Then, shame. For not being able to predict that my 'ignoring', better known as reading, would upset her so much. I made a mental note that in future, I shouldn't get so engrossed in my book and should check on her more regularly.

Then a wave of irritability came over me. 'If she wanted a chat, why didn't she just call out to me?' I wondered. My guilt dissipated, and I went back to reading my book.

XXX

The envy of a covert narcissist is imperceptible. We will never see it unless we're willing to look beneath the charade.

*So Machiavellian is the narcissistic personality, that even when they succeed in controlling another person, it's not enough. They need to see their victim suffer. They need to see some form of resistance...... (And compliance....... at the same time!) Compliance makes them feel powerful, but if the victim has found a way of being comfortable in their compliance (like I did by staying home and reading), this irks them. They need conflict.*

# Chapter 31 - My saving grace

In my early teens, I discovered that I was good at drama. The Mothers' response to my newfound talent was a combination of ridicule and dismissiveness.

I rationalised her disappointment and assumed it was because drama is less academic than other subjects. I believed her to be 'cruel to be kind'. I convinced myself that she worried this talent wouldn't get me very far in life. I thought her withholding of support was borne out of genuine concern for my future. The tales we spin when under the spell of a narcissist! Despite my social anxiety, I tried to prove to her that I could excel in life by excelling in this subject. I was attracted to the idea of pretending I was someone else. I could play at being angry, mean, and boisterous and explore emotions I wouldn't dare to in real life. The freedom of expression was liberating and intoxicating.

I had secretly wanted to go to stage school for a while but knew asking The Mother was pointless. I decided to find my own way into the field, starting with GCSE drama.

I revealed my choice to her at Options evening. I was perhaps hoping that she would be less prickly in public. She wasn't. She was immediately scornful, telling me that I wasn't 'allowed' to choose Drama. When I probed for a logical rationale, she couldn't articulate one. So, I knew that she was simply saying I couldn't because I wanted to. It was about control. Again.

However, I knew that she didn't have the energy, or self-discipline to follow through with what was a nonsensical knee-jerk reaction. So, I said nothing and bided my time again. Then, I chose Drama, with no further discussion from her.

Shortly after my secret determination to become an actress, The Mother decided that I should change schools again. After three years, she decided that this school was also not good enough. She seemed to think that I should be able to achieve straight A's if the school was doing their job properly. This, despite also telling me frequently how stupid I was!

I don't think she moved me because she was disappointed with my grades. (Which were average.) I think she moved me because I was finally happier, and I now had friends I was socialising with on Saturday afternoons.

She moved me to my third secondary school at the start of my GCSEs. Ironically, she moved me to a school where I found the best, most supportive and encouraging drama teacher. After my first drama lesson, he asked me to audition for the school play, which I did, after which he offered me a supporting actress role.

She told me I wasn't allowed to participate because I'd be coming home too late. (This school was also an hour and a half away from home.) My drama teacher then made an irresistible offer. He would drive me home after every rehearsal day. She could find no reason to say no.

If she'd just isolated me, without convincing me that her motive in changing my school, and pushing me academically, was altruistic, I might have rebelled. But I was well and truly brainwashed. Even though I didn't feel loved by her, I still believed that she wanted the best for me. So, I worked harder than ever, trying to prove my worth by excelling in drama. I became dedicated to rehearsing for the school play every night. Being so busy, it was easy to ignore her disinterest. I hoped that once she saw me on stage and saw the reaction from the audience, she'd realise that I could be something.

Dutifully, she came to see me one night in the play. But after the performance, she said nothing. I noticed her hypocrisy. She said she wanted me to excel, and here I was, excelling. In front of everyone. This shy, introverted, anxious girl who wouldn't say boo to a goose came alive on stage. I knew from the audience's reaction, of about 200 people, that I'd done well.

Her reaction was a stark contrast that made no sense. I didn't dare ask her opinion, though, because I assumed her silence was because she didn't think I was very good. At least, that's what she was trying to make me think. In reality, I now believe her silence conveyed anger and envy. Anger at the fact that I'd found something I was good at. And envy because others showered me with praise and compliments.

The following year, I played the lead. She fulfilled her parental obligation by coming to see the show again, this time with her boyfriend. Afterwards, he took us to dinner; I thought to celebrate the show's success. It was our last performance after a four-night run, so I was euphoric. Dinner brought me down to earth with a bang. There was no celebrating. There was barely any mention of the play except for The Mother saying how talented and pretty my co-stars were. There was no mention of my performance.

XXX

My focus on drama was beneficial in distracting me from the daily bullying I was enduring from a gang of eight girls. For almost two years, they tormented me, following me, harassing me, verbally abusing and threatening me. One day as I walked past a building site, they even started throwing rocks at me on the way home. I ignored it all. This was the advice from The Mother years ago. To ignore it, and it would go away. But it didn't. It got worse. One day, I couldn't take it anymore, and I told my drama teacher.

He must have called her because when I got home, she questioned me. It was like a valve loosened. The pressure of two years of anger, frustration, fear and sadness suddenly erupted in an overflow of emotion. She didn't offer any words of comfort, but it was a relief that I could finally talk about it.

I went to my bedroom feeling a bit lighter, when I overheard her saying to my younger sister that I was 'making a big deal out of it.' I was crushed. I never confronted her about what she said, but I knew then that the concern she'd just shown was fake.

XXX

She never thanked my drama teacher for driving me home all those nights. Nor did she ever offer to contribute to his petrol. As a 14-year-old, such things didn't occur to me. But as an adult, I feel embarrassed on her behalf.

In hindsight, I think the reason for her ignorant ungrateful behaviour towards my teacher was twofold. It demonstrates both her entitlement and resentment. The Mother never says 'thank you' for anything. And she wouldn't have liked a teacher, or anyone for that matter, showing me positive attention. So, she ignored him as a form of protest.

*Narcissists don't respond well when their victims get attention from others. It likely triggers the usual array of emotions. Envy, rage and frustration.*

# Chapter 32 - Narcissists minimise our accomplishments

The Mother seemed to resent interacting with me, so she did so with animosity most of the time, especially if we were alone. The animosity increased around household tasks. I always thought she feared I'd revolt. So, she began the tasks immediately with aggression. She huffed and puffed, swore and shouted, whilst I meekly took orders. My compliance didn't make things easier. She'd rage throughout the whole process, regardless. It was the same every weekend for years.

Weekly laundry sessions involved me standing silently, holding a hose, whilst enduring her two-hour tirade of abuse about how useless, stupid and lazy I was.

Despite my participation in household chores, I never learned any skills. She refused to teach me. Whenever I tried to show interest or ask questions, her stock response was, 'you should know, you go to school'. I knew at the time this was an ill-fitting response. I knew it was passive-aggressive, and that she was withholding knowledge and support from me, but I still felt stupid for asking. It had the desired effect. I stopped asking questions. I tried to get through the rest of my life without knowing what I needed to know.

One Saturday, my brother came by. In hindsight, it seems that she'd orchestrated the conversation that followed. She recruited him as a flying monkey, it seems. (A step up from being the scapegoat, for him.)

She asked me in front of him why I chose Drama. Asking me questions about my life goals?! What a rare occurrence!

"Where did I hope this would lead to?" She asked in a condescending tone. Naively I tried to defend my choice, honestly. Thinking logic would win her over.

"Actors do make a living. It is a real job", I said. She responded that actors are attractive people, and I 'don't have the face for it.' I pointed out that lots of actors don't look like models. That was my brother's cue to 'talk some sense' into me. He jumped on her bandwagon, asking, "How many people do you think apply for drama school every year? What makes you think they would choose you?"

He didn't know whether I was talented or not. He'd never seen me perform in anything. So, I immediately disregarded what he said internally; whilst being careful not to display this outwardly. Her cruel jabs and his presumptions didn't deter me.

She dug the knife deeper when she knew she wasn't making a dent in my hopes and dreams. She looked at me with pity. "Sure, you know I'm only for your good. Wouldn't you rather hear it from me than from someone else? You're not pretty enough to be on TV."

Even when I'd finally found something I enjoyed, she succeeded in making me feel shame about it. She tried her hardest to convince me that I wasn't good enough. Rejecting my talent as meaningless because it wasn't what she wanted me to be good at.

Of course, now I know that whatever subject I may have been good at, she would have been compelled to reject it because narcissistic mothers are envious of their children's accomplishments.

The joy I found in my discovered talent was, of course, dampened by her reaction. She seemed as embarrassed of my love for drama as if I'd said I wanted to be a prostitute or a porn star!

Although I found her embarrassment confusing and odd, I still internalised it and shied away from sharing my hopes and dreams with others, fearing they'd mock me too.

My drama teacher was sure I was talented enough to get into drama school and frequently gave up some of his lunch breaks to rehearse my audition pieces with me.

XXX

Her minimising of all our accomplishments are an inherent part of her Narcissistic Personality Disorder. She has to destroy everyone's successes and dreams because acknowledging them would make her feel less than.

*\* Another frame of reference, such as a teacher or other adult in our life, can provide the perspective we need to give us a peak into reality - the truth that our narcissistic parent's version of the world, and us, is not real.\**

# Chapter 33 - The narcissist abandons, despite this being their greatest fear

In my mid-teens, she took to spending weekends away with her boyfriend. After a few times, the thought suddenly occurred to me that I was free. It hit me like a slap in the face. What was I doing, following her stupid rules in her absence?!

I'm embarrassed that my mind didn't go to parties, alcohol or dating like a typical teenager. I excitedly thought, 'I could have a cup of tea if I wanted to! Mmm! And chips! I could have chips!!'

I'd almost succeeded. The homemade chips were just about ready to eat, and the tea had just been poured when the front door swung open. (I'd made the mistake of leaving the kitchen and porch doors open so she could see right into the kitchen from the front door.)

She froze, staring at me with a big grin on her face. Perhaps she was surprised to see me breaking her rules.

I panicked; turning my back to her. I squeezed out the tea bag from the cup, with my hands shaking. As I shoved the scalding tea bag down my knickers, I poured the tea down the sink, hoping I'd acted fast enough for her not to notice. There was nothing I could do about the chips. I was busted with that.

My heart was pounding, and my nether regions were scalding! I must have looked like a rabbit caught in headlights. Strangely she didn't react. Other than the startled grin she was wearing.

Although I don't remember him being with her, I know he was. She didn't do anything for herself if she could help it. He chauffeured her everywhere. She never mentioned the warm kettle or the chips just made, but that was the end of the 'no tea and chips allowed' phase.

XXX

It never occurred to me until I started writing this book that she presented a different mask to her boyfriend. That of 'the little woman.' She was subservient to him. Even when he wasn't being nice to her. For six years, I never saw her show him the side of her that I knew. The person who shouts mantras, sulks, blames and rages. He had no idea who she was. I think she didn't react when she saw me breaking her rules because of her need to keep this act up in front of him.

XXX

Most of the abuse committed by narcissistic parents is hard to prove in a court of law because it is mostly about subliminal manipulation and distorting reality. However, she did break the law more than once in various ways. But because she'd caused me such brain fog, I didn't even know when she was breaking the law. But, even if I did know, there would have been no one to tell.

She'd been talking for years of her fantasy of running away with her boyfriend to Ireland and hiring someone to finish raising my younger sister and I. She never took any action to implement this plan. It was just something she ruminated on.

I was still in school when she and her boyfriend left us at home alone to go on holiday. Before leaving, there was no discussion about what to do in an emergency. She didn't leave enough food or money for the duration either. Our older siblings could have looked out for us during this time, but she didn't tell them that she'd left the country.

One time, a few years ago, I saw a news report of a mother that was charged with neglect for going on holiday and leaving her child at home alone. For the first time, I thought, 'Oh! That was illegal?!'

She was such an opposing force that I was relieved to be rid of her. Thinking about basic needs like food and safety didn't occur to me. Until I realised there wasn't enough food, and we weren't safe. Not having enough to eat turned out to be the least of our worries. Unfortunately for us, she chose to communicate with us once by postcard. Suddenly, a creepy postman started paying us both extra attention. He let us know he knew we were alone. "Your mum having a nice holiday?"

We were both nervous around this man. It scared us that he knew there was no adult in the home. I wasn't angry that we had to get jobs to feed ourselves. I wasn't even hurt or angry that she couldn't be bothered to ring us. But I was furious with her for putting us in this potential danger.

It seemed that he was watching the house. We got this impression because he'd start to frequently bump into us 'accidentally' to strike up a conversation.

He only backed off once she'd returned. The naivety of her behaviour was what stayed with me. 'The old dog for the long road?' yeah, right! (This was a mantra she used often. It meant, no matter how old or knowledgeable you get, I will always be older than you; therefore, I will always know more than you.)

The Mother longed to be free of us. But at the same time, she used us as the reason why she couldn't commit fully to her boyfriend. Despite wishing for him to rescue her from the boredom and responsibility of being a parent, she also didn't want the responsibility of being a wife. She used him, just like she used us.

*Narcissists tend to attract enablers that encourage and support their behaviour.*

# Chapter 34 - Narcissists sabotage their victim's success

The Mother suddenly lost interest in my education at the most crucial moment. When Year 11 ('5th year' at the time) 'study leave' came around, she grew more irritated by my presence because I was now home during the day. She didn't seem to understand that it was a critical time for me. She didn't seem to understand that the purpose of 'study leave' was to revise for exams. She started treating me like an unemployed lodger who'd stopped paying rent. I'd get up daily to a list of chores, including home renovations. The list got longer and longer each day, and I wasn't allowed to revise it until the list was completed. She started to repeat the mantra, 'you need to start paying your way'. I was busy revising throughout the night, sometimes until 5 am, to achieve what I wanted and what she wanted.

She never knew what exams I was taking or when they were. She never asked. One morning during my chores, I couldn't help becoming visibly irritable. My exam was fast approaching, and I'd miss it if I didn't get ready soon. I tried to explain this to her, but she became verbally abusive. The chore was not allowed to be left, I had to do it 'NOW'.

So, I did it with silent resentment. Then I darted out the front door without saying goodbye. I was angry that she seemed to think the chore (that could easily have been done later or by her) was more important than the exam I'd spent all night revising for. Luckily, I made it. I was hot, sweaty and dishevelled, but I made it.

On my walk home after the exam, we happened to cross paths. She cycled up from behind me, looking annoyed.

"What was wrong with you this morning?"

"Mum, I had an exam, and I almost missed it. You nearly made me late."

"Oh. I thought you were just being a bitch'". She cycled off.

Years later, this pain resurfaced when I saw friends support their children through their exams. I remembered that even though I lived in her house, I was going through the experience alone during my exams.

I watched my friends being fully invested in their children's education. Texting them good luck before exams, knowing exactly what exam they were doing each day. Excitedly calling immediately afterwards, wanting to know all the details about how their child thought they did.

The unresolved trauma I'd long since buried was awakened. (At the time of my exams, I didn't feel the pain of her disinterest because I didn't know it was abnormal. I knew it was unreasonable, but I didn't know that she secretly wanted me to fail. I didn't know that she was deliberately trying to sabotage my success. Even though I felt angry and frustrated with her, she'd convinced me that I had no business being in her house if I was of no use to her.)

Despite her sabotage, I did OK. Not great, but OK. I opened the results at home, alone, and cried with joy when I saw my A for Drama. It was the only subject I cared about, so I wasn't disappointed with seven GCSEs, an A, a B and five C's. It was enough to progress, and I excelled in what I cared about. However, without asking what my results were, she insisted that I should re-sit every subject until I got all A's.

So, I returned to school and told my teachers I would be re-sitting. A couple of them tried to talk me out of it. One said that very few people do better when they retake. He said that if I'd tried my hardest, which I did, I would likely get the same results again. My drama teacher said, 'No one retakes their GCSEs if they've got enough to go further because once you go further, no one cares what the GCSE results are.'

However, I was so under The Mother's influence that I disregarded my teachers' advice and re-sat subjects I'd already passed. I didn't ask why she wanted me to retake; I just knew she was disappointed in me....again. And I wanted to please her.

I was now two years behind my peers. This further damaged my self-esteem, because re-sitting is humiliating. It took me decades to realise that this was another act of academic sabotage. (The first being putting me back a year in school.)

*Success and achievements present another double bind for the child of a narcissist. We don't understand that our success and achievements threaten them because they are secretly competing with us. Of course, if we fail, we're also a disappointment. So, there's no solution. There's no changing the script on our part, no matter how much we try. That's a right reserved exclusively for the narcissist.*

# Chapter 35 - The narcissist's ever-changing script

Growing up, The Mother made it clear that she wanted a quiet, obedient child. She didn't like a child who asked questions or sought attention. I gave her exactly what she wanted. I had consciously, to some extent, forgone my right to develop and express my personality. I never answered back. I never had a tantrum. I never said 'no' (at least not directly.) I never asked anything from her. I gave up authenticity to meet her needs. This process was difficult and painful because I did have a strong sense of self. To know it but not be allowed to express it was invalidating and depressing. But I'd been playing this role of emotional servitude for so long that it had become me.

After she spent time with a friend of hers, and her child one evening, she attempted to regale me with tales of how wonderful this child was. He wasn't quiet or obedient. He was the exact opposite. Gregarious, loud, attention-seeking even. All things she'd previously despised.

Yet, overnight, she changed her mind like a kid in a sweet shop. She seemed to expect me to be able to immediately transform my personality, at will, to meet her new demands.

This was a tactic I'd grown used to. Whatever she wanted me to do, she would try to manipulate into doing it by telling me how much better she or someone else did it.

When she said, 'Sure, when I was your age, I'd turn around and clean the whole house', it meant 'cleaning your room isn't good enough. I want you to clean the whole house.' And later, 'Sure, when I was your age, I'd be sending most of my wages home to my mother,' meant 'I'd like you to give me most of your wages'. So, 'He was so funny and cute!' I knew meant 'Why can't you be funny and cute?'

I didn't understand how she could have this rapport, this fondness for someone else's child, when nothing could make her like her own children.

As I got older, her demand for me to morph into something other than myself continued. Before her boyfriend came along, she'd aggressively shamed me into acting as if I was asexual. She did this by frequently throwing out baseless random accusations of my supposed lasciviousness. She seemed to think I was so lustful that I was planning to have sex with any boy as soon as the opportunity presented itself.

I now understand that shaming me into acting asexual was a way of preventing me from trying to develop relationships with others. Once she'd successfully manoeuvred me into the position of pretending I was asexual, she started to shame me for it. With her boyfriend's influence, she swung from one end of the pendulum to the other. From requiring me to be nun-like to demanding that I act like a raving nymphomaniac! All because her boyfriend decided that I wasn't 'normal'. She told me he'd said I 'should be breaking down the door to get out, (to meet boys) at (my) age'.

Not long after her demands changed, she told me that she had a nightmare that a man I met on holiday (I was 15. He was 25....) came to the house in the middle of the night to move me out. She was so affected by the dream that she got up to check that it wasn't real.

At the time, I didn't know what to make of it. Now, I understand it was a manifestation of her greatest fear – that someone would help me escape from her.

## XXX

Having to wear a false mask often presents a challenge for the narcissist. They're often caught between a rock and a hard place. She couldn't let her boyfriend know she wanted me to act asexual, so I'd always be under her thumb. That would sound weird!

*Narcissists express what they 'like' or 'dislike' based on what those they idealise like and dislike. This is why their opinions often are fickle and contradictory.*

# Chapter 36 - 'You can fuck off out of here when you're 16'......

Was a mantra The Mother used a lot, randomly with no context. She'd been saying this since I was about six. Along with other mantras like, 'I had four children, and not one of ye turned out any good' and 'breeding beats feeding' (meaning that I was like my dad no matter how much she tried to make me not like him.)I never argued when she spat out these mantras. I just absorbed them. They had the effect of brainwashing me. Her opinions of me became my opinions of me. It wasn't until after I'd deprogrammed myself that I realised that the other outcome of her rehearsed mantras was that they kept me at arms-length. It's impossible to have a two-way interaction with this communication style. It prevents emotional intimacy.

As my 16th birthday approached, I started thinking about how I'd survive. (The year I finished my GCSE's, I was, in fact, 17, so I was well aware that I'd outstayed my welcome.)

Despite wanting me to re-sit my GCSEs, she made it clear that she wouldn't be financially supporting me through the process. I needed to take my re-sits whilst living independently. She never gave me a date to leave home directly; she just stepped up the pressure for me to go. I was of no use by this point. My younger sister didn't need babysitting anymore.

I worked full-time in a jewellery factory during the summer

holidays to save for a deposit. But, even the amount of time it took to accumulate this was irritating to her. She no longer wanted me at home in the evenings.

One night, when I got in from work, she said it wasn't 'normal for a young girl to spend every night in.'

Don't I have any friends? She asked. "Other young girls are out on the town, and you come in the house every evening like you've got nothing better to do."

I didn't have anything better to do. And she knew that. My friends were in Edgware, and I was in Harlesden. It wouldn't have been worth the time and money to travel by public transport to meet up with them after work.

But there was another reason I was avoiding my friends. There was another reason I was so obedient around The Mother's non-dating rules. It was becoming clear that I didn't want to date boys. I was starting to realise I was gay.

Although I didn't know what 'gay' was. I just thought I was a freak of nature, an oddity. The only one in the world. I had no idea that there was such a thing as gay people, or a 'gay scene.' So I was terrified of my feelings.

My first plan was to 'pray the gay away.' One night, I got out of bed and knelt, 'Please God, make these feelings go away. I don't want them. Thank you.'

When the prayers had no effect, I moved on to Plan B. To take my secret to the grave. I felt shame and terror at being found out, which increased my self-loathing. 'As if she didn't have enough reasons not to love me?!' I thought. My big concern became how to keep this secret. I imagined having to live a fake life. However, the thought of pretending, and marrying a man to save face, made me feel suicidal.

I kept my secret by distancing myself from those I knew. I attempted to cure this self-imposed loneliness by reaching out to gay social groups. I started buying Time Out magazine and took to circling various groups of interest.

One evening I got careless and left the magazine on my desk in my bedroom, whilst I went downstairs to make a cup of tea. She entered the kitchen, shortly afterwards, where I was watching TV, and turned it off to get my full attention. She looked at me with a horrified expression. She'd found my magazine whilst snooping. Her face looked as if she'd caught me red-handed, dipping into her purse or something!

Her new obsession became trying to un-gay me. She sat me down and told me she didn't believe I was gay, just lonely. That all I needed to do was find the right man. I tried to insist that I knew I was gay, but she wouldn't hear anything I had to say.

She insisted on writing an advert for a lonely-hearts column on my behalf. I sat silently, motionless and helpless, whilst she wrote out the advert and cheque. It seemed easier to let her believe that she could change me rather than argue.

I posted the letter, like she told me to. I look back now and think, why didn't I just pretend, then say it must have got lost in the post? The thought didn't occur to me.

When the responses returned, I was shocked by how inappropriate they were. Some were from way older men, in their 50s. One offered to take me to Ireland with him!

Only one was in his 20's, so she selected him. Under her command, I wrote back to him, and we met up. Once. Her attempts at trying to un-gay me fizzled out after that.

XXX

A silent tension grew between her boyfriend and I, with him dropping hints that he knew I was gay. He provocatively started calling me by a boy's name, trying to shame and provoke me.

With his support, her hostility towards my sexuality grew more overt. She shouted at me down the street that I 'look like a right fucking dyke now' the day I returned from the hairdressers with a short haircut. I was perplexed more than anything and slightly amused that she didn't mind letting the whole street know I was gay, despite claiming that it embarrassed her so much!

She now had the ammunition she needed to blame me for her

discarding of me. My being gay validated her kicking me out.

She used triangulation to express her 'concern' that my younger sister could be 'at risk' from me. I tried to explain that being gay and being a sexual predator wasn't the same. Although she never conceded that this is true, she changed tactic, saying that my younger sister 'may be influenced' by me, and she didn't want that to happen. So I had to go.

Once I'd saved enough for a deposit and a week's rent upfront (about £420 at the time), I told her I'd found a room. She looked at me with a smug expression. "You'll move out when I tell you to!!" (A counsellor once told me a crazy person could drive a sane person crazy!)

Despite this confusing response, she and her boyfriend helped me pack his car with my few belongings, including a 'put-you-up bed' for the floor. They dropped me at the room around 9 p.m.

I don't remember the conversation in the car, and I don't remember there being any palpable tension. I suspect she was happy that I was no longer her responsibility, which is why she may have been so helpful.

However, after we'd unloaded the car and said our goodbyes, she suddenly started crying. This unexpected emotion was upsetting and confusing for me. This move wasn't what I wanted. It was what she wanted. Yet, in a split second, she was able to reverse things and make me feel guilty. As if I was abandoning her! It seemed that no matter what, she would always find a way to be hurt by me. I became tearful because I couldn't bear to see the pain I was causing her.

After I shut the door and looked at the small dark room with walls full of mould, I wished we could have had an honest conversation. I wished I could run outside and stop the car and tell her that I'm not trying to hurt her. That I thought she wanted me to leave. That I don't want to live in this room all by myself. I'm scared!

Why isn't she happy? I thought later that night as I cried myself to sleep quietly. Why didn't she say so if she didn't want me to leave?

I'll never know if she suddenly felt sad or if they were crocodile tears. I know they made no sense, given the history of our relationship. Now that I reflect on my knowledge, I suspect she felt out of control at that moment. So, she got upset. The Mother controls others. It makes her feel better. So, as much as she didn't want me around, she liked to control me. It made her feel powerful.

Discarding me was a double-edged sword that perhaps she didn't think through. She couldn't possibly have the same control over me she'd always had now that I was no longer living at home. Perhaps this loss of control was what she was grieving.

*In the self-help book 'Children of Emotionally Immature Parents, author Lyndsey C. Gibson refers to the 'rejecting' kind of parent, who 'seems not to want to spend time with their children and seem happiest if (they're left) alone.' The children get the feeling (their parents would be) fine if they didn't exist.*

## Chapter 37 - Freedom wasn't what I thought it would be

I had no idea how unequipped I was for a life of independence. I didn't know how to open a bank account. I didn't know how to drive. I didn't know how to cook a meal. I didn't even know how to tidy my room! But being a teenager, none of this phased me because, as the saying goes, 'you don't know what you don't know until you know it.'

In the weeks before leaving home, all I could think of was being free of her. I fantasised about being able to eat what I want, wear what I wanted, and I imagined having the freedom to go out with friends and date. Of course, none of this became a reality. The responsibility of paying rent, whilst resitting exams, weighed heavy on me.

I took a part-time evening and weekend job at Sainsbury's and an early morning paper round. This paid the rent, but I lived on expensive ready meals, without knowing how to cook. Often resulting in insufficient food for the week. One day all I had was Weetabix, so I ate it for breakfast, lunch and dinner. I've not been able to eat it since.

I started to become resentful of The Mother, for continuing to collect child benefits. I resented my older colleagues for earning more than me for the same job, and I resented my friends for living everyday teenage life. So, I distanced myself further from everyone to hide these uncomfortable feelings.

It was stressful not knowing how to do anything for myself, and having no one to ask for help. As a result I became reclusive.

I was only in school a few months before I realised that my teachers were right. Repeating was a waste of time. I wasn't doing any better than I did in the summer.

As The Mother had predicted many times with the mantra 'You'll never amount to anything,' I became a dropout.

In hindsight, I suspect she was envious of my drive to succeed. Pushing me academically was only fun for her, whilst I had no interest. Once I had goals of my own and encouragement from a teacher………. this was not in her plans!

So, I believe discarding me was another (3rd) act of academic sabotage. An attempt to prevent me from going further in my education. And she succeeded. For the next three years, at least.

*The typical cycle of narcissistic relationships is 'Love Bombing – Devaluing – Discarding – Hoovering back – before the Final discard'. It's also common for narcissists to never give closure. To keep someone at arm's length, and do just enough in the way of breadcrumbing, to keep them around for when they need them. This became the essence of my relationship with The Mother.*

# Chapter 38 - Co-dependency

The pain a narcissistic abuser causes is indistinguishable from their victims' concept of love. This amalgamation of love and pain causes an addictive, toxic, co-dependent dynamic in which the victim unwittingly becomes complicit in their abuse. It's what's known as the trauma bond. (What used to be known as Stockholm Syndrome.)

With a combination of breadcrumbing, projection and gaslighting, they convince their victim that they are the perpetrator. They set us up for a cycle of repeatedly trying to prove that we're not the awful abuser they perceive us to be. It is as if our life and worth depend on their validation.

XXX

Despite The Mother's rejection of me, I visited her regularly. I hoped that by no longer being a burden to her, we might finally develop a better relationship.

One afternoon we played badminton together. I don't know what possessed me, but during the game, I suddenly had the urge to say, "It feels like nobody loves me". She responded in a strained tone of voice. As if she was trying to force incredulity.

"Nobody loves you? Nobody loves you?!" It was a weird tone that signalled, 'you're being ridiculous.' I didn't push any further. We played the rest of the game in silence.

She took herself off swimming five minutes after I'd arrived on another visit. I was so used to her doing weird stuff like this that the rudeness of it, and the message she was sending me, fell on deaf ears. I amused myself with TV until her return.

She charged into the house like a whirlwind, insisting that I immediately leave the house with her. As she was rushing back out the door, she told me to hurry up, to get my bike and follow her. I did, repeatedly asking, "What's going on? Where are we going? What's the matter? What's happening?"

"Come on…. Hurry up for God's Sake!" She shouted back at me as I tried to cycle faster to keep up with her.

"Get a move on!……. You can go faster than that!……. Peddle faster!….. Sure, you're younger than me, and ye can't keep up! …… Come on!"

Like a fool, I followed her even though she was stonewalling me. Twenty minutes later, we arrived at a building I'd never been to. As we got off our bikes, out of breath, I continued to ask questions as I followed her.

"Mum, what is it? What are we doing here?"

We were at an aerobics class. She walked me into the class, then turned on her heels swiftly and walked out. But not before turning back to give me a flash of her false teeth. She looked proud that she'd dragged me here to participate in a class without my knowledge or consent. I didn't have the guts to walk out, though. That felt too confrontational.

So, I took the class resentfully and never challenged The Mother on her behaviour, because I was scared of her. She had a vicious tongue, and any questioning of her would have been seen as an attack and, therefore, a valid excuse to attack back. At least by allowing myself to be controlled, I evaded her verbal abuse.

*Victims of narcissists often become co-dependent. They are setting us up for a lifetime of abuse by other narcissists. We only see the toxicity of the narcissist/co-dependent dynamic when we're provided with another frame of reference.*

# Chapter 39 - Self-abandonment

My 16th, 17th and 18th passed without celebration or acknowledgement. Not even from myself. I spent much of my late teens, and early 20's alone and depressed in rented rooms, moving around a lot, trying to escape from myself. My social anxiety became so bad that I could no longer interact spontaneously with others. I developed an obsessive-compulsive habit of rehearsing what I wanted to say in my mind before I would allow myself to speak. I felt that every sentence had to be perfect so that nothing could be misconstrued, mocked, or criticised. Often by the time I felt ready to speak, the conversation had moved on. No one had any idea of the internal battle I was struggling with.

By my late teens, this severe social anxiety morphed into selective mutism. The thought that made me stop talking was 'Nobody gives a fuck what I think or feel, so there's no point in speaking'. I had been trapped in this selective mutism for three years before the same thought led to me talking again. It was the same thought but from a different perspective. 'Nobody gives a fuck what I think or feel……..so no one is coming to rescue me. No one cares. If I'm ever going to live a normal life, I will have to get myself out of this'. And just like that, I began talking again. The Mother acted like she didn't notice I'd gone mute. She also acted like she didn't notice I'd started speaking again.

The belief that led to my social anxiety, and later to selective mutism, was based on her projection powers. As a narcissist, she projected her boredom outwards, blaming me for the hollowness of our relationship. As a brainwashed co-dependent, I readily internalised her projections.

Despite this and my ongoing loneliness and isolation, I still had dreams and the motivation to chase them. At 19, I got into drama school. A prestigious one at that. However, shortly after getting my acceptance letter, my anxiety got the better of me. Instead of being excited to start my new life, I dreaded the approaching September.

Admission day came and went. A year later, I got myself onto a BTEC Performing Arts course. With the help of an acquaintance, I also managed to get into a homeless hostel, which meant that I could pay a reduced rent.

I did well in the first year, winning the 'Most Improved Student award.' The Mother stroked my face when I told her. Beaming that, "We'll make something out of ye yet." This fleeting moment of maternal pride felt like unicorns, buttercups, Disneyland, rainbows, candy floss, bunny rabbits and puppies all rolled into one!

I spent decades trying to recreate this moment. For years I believed this to be a glimpse of her true self. Proof that there was something worth fighting for. There wasn't.

Despite doing well in college and having a friend, my depression and social anxiety worsened. Nine months after my 21st birthday, I tried to take my life.

Not long before, The Mother had told me that she'd rather I was dead than gay because at least if I were dead, her friends and family would feel sorry for her. She said that if people found out I was gay; they'd think it was because she was a bad mother.

I concluded that the only way I could please her was to kill myself. I sincerely believed giving up my life for her happiness was the right thing to do.

I imagined that I'd be going to hell for being gay, anyway, so my logic was, 'What's the point in being alive for years, trying to be a good person? If when you die, you're going to go to hell anyway because you're gay?' I thought it made sense to take the shortcut and be done with it.

I'd been planning my suicide for two weeks. I told different people various stories about where I'd be, so that by the time I'd be found, it would be too late.

It was a cold October morning when I gathered together my suicide kit. I didn't want questions to be asked, so I collected several packets of paracetamol, razor blades and cans of beer from various shops. My plan was to overdose. A method I imagined would be easy. I'd get drowsy, drift into unconsciousness, then die.

However, I had a backup plan, just in case overdosing wasn't as easy as I thought. Perhaps I would need to cut my wrists as well. I'd heard that alcohol numbs pain, so I planned on drinking through the process.

I walked into a toilet of a local library and locked the door. Before I started to swallow the pills, I wrote a suicide note. It read something like, 'I know I'm not what you wanted. You didn't deserve a daughter like me. I'm sorry I can't be who you want me to be. I want you to know that despite how disappointing I am to you, I do love you unconditionally. I know I'm not good enough for you to love back, but I want you to know that I will do anything to make you happy. Since this is the only thing I can do, I am happy to take my life. If it means pleasing you. Now you'll no longer have to endure the embarrassment of my existence. You're free to be happy. I go to hell knowing I did the right thing for us both.'

I imagined her fake crying at my funeral. Eliciting all the sympathy, she coveted. Whilst secretly smiling inside, thinking, 'thank you, Charlie. Now I know you did love me.'

I read my suicide note, ripped it into small pieces and flushed it down the toilet. I didn't want people to blame The Mother for my actions.

I opened a can of beer, took out some tablets, and washed them down until I started retching. In between retching, I tried to swallow more. I could only swallow one or two more before it became impossible. In total, I swallowed about 50.

The stomach ache that quickly followed was excruciating. I

remember thinking, 'this must mean I's working'.

I lay down, closed my eyes, and longed for death. I imagined drifting into nothingness. I had some fear, but I wanted it to be over more than anything. To not exist. I started drifting in and out of consciousness in between bouts of vomiting.

After several hours I thought, 'this isn't working'. So, I took out the razor blade and ran it across my wrist. It was harder to cut and hurt more than I expected. Eventually, I gave up on the wrist and started cutting my arms. The sensation of blood oozing out was releasing.

At some point, I slipped into unconsciousness only to be roused by a loud banging on the toilet door. A man shouted that the library was closing. It was 8 pm. I'd been there since 9 am.

Here I was. Not dead. Feeling rough but not dead. I drifted out into the cold dark air. I wasn't well enough to walk anywhere.

I felt that death was slowly approaching. I just needed to lie down until it came. I chose a spot behind some bushes, hoping the darkness would make me inconspicuous to passers-by. I tucked behind them, trying to avoid thorns, and lay down on the cold soil. I closed my eyes, hoping to die of hyperthermia.

But, still, death didn't come. I looked at my watch. It was midnight. My hostel was a 15-minute walk away. The Mother lived 30 minutes away. I chose to walk to her house. I don't remember why. Perhaps I was scared. Maybe I wanted her to know that I'd tried but failed to please her.

She was always a light sleeper. So, she answered the door immediately. She didn't seem shocked that I showed up at her house at 12.30 am. She turned her back and walked into her bedroom without asking why I was there. I followed her.

I sat down on her bed and told her that I'd failed in trying to kill myself. She didn't seem shocked, upset or angry. She just seemed tired.

"It's late. You can sleep upstairs. Your bed's made up." I went up to my old bedroom and slept peacefully.

I woke feeling surprisingly ok, physically. I had some mild palpitations but no nausea.

I went downstairs in a dressing gown I'd left behind. The Mother was already up and pottering around in the kitchen. She seemed calm like she was last night.

Not long after, my younger sister appeared in the lounge. The Mother suddenly grabbed my arm where the open bloody self-harm wounds were visible. She dug her fingernails into the fresh sore cuts and pulled me close, snarling, "If you want to feel pain, I'll give you pain". My eyes filled with tears. I looked over her shoulder to see my sister's eyes also filled with tears.

XXX

I believe that she suddenly became self-conscious of her uncaring behaviour in the presence of a witness. So, she did what she always did when caught out. She acted her way out of it.

Her immediate go-to was always to make me feel guilty by pretending to be hurt by my behaviour. But this time, because I knew she wasn't genuinely hurt, it came off as odd and intimidating. She made no pretence of being upset with me the previous night or that morning before there was a witness.

XXX

When I realised, I wasn't going to die from the first attempt, I immediately planned to try again. I made my second suicide attempt about a week later. This time, I didn't bother to tell anyone that I'd failed afterwards.

*Dr Ramani on YouTube refers to **Social Anxiety, Social Phobia** and **Selective Mutism** as responses to the lack of safety involved in being around a narcissist long term. She explains that 'all conversations are like being in a maze.' There's no way out. The list gets longer and longer of what we can't talk about, what will offend etc., so it's not safe to be spontaneous.*

## Chapter 40 - Narcissists invent reasons to punish their victim

When my parents divorced, my dad opened an account of £100 balance for each of his children. The Mother was the gatekeeper of these accounts. At 18, we were allowed access to our funds on her say-so. Although I knew of this, it wasn't something I ever really thought about.

Two years after my younger sister turned of age, The Mother let me know, seemingly in passing, that she gave her access to her money on her 18th. She'd already prevented me from accessing my account for four years.

In response to her revelation, I asked if I could access my account too. She screamed at me in a high street so loudly that others stopped and stared. "You're fucking obsessed with money'" She then withheld it for several months because I'd dared to ask for it.

Eventually, I got the money. With it, I decided to fulfil a dream I'd been discussing since I was 12. I was going to start a new life in America. When I got there, I had no idea what to do, but being a naïve 22-year-old, I thought the world was my oyster. Perhaps I would find fame and fortune like Madonna when she rocked up to Times Square in New York with $35 in her purse!

She did everything she could to deter me from my dream, telling me how unsafe New York is and how impossible it would be to get a green card. Then one morning, only a few weeks before I was due to leave, she told me about her friend's daughter, who wasn't much older than myself. She'd gone to the US and opened a successful hairdressing salon. She gushed over how intelligent and courageous her friend's daughter was for making a new life in America. When I asked why she'd tried so hard to discourage me when she was happy for someone else to achieve what was my dream, she just chuckled.

XXX

Again, I thought by escaping my life; I could escape myself; that I could become a different person in a different environment. But alas, my depression and anxiety followed me. After ten months in LA, I returned to The Mother's home broke. It was only a matter of weeks before she started to make me feel unwelcome again, despite hardly ever seeing me. (I was working like crazy to move out as fast as possible. As a dishwasher in a restaurant until 2 am, and a cleaner in a hardware store from 7 am.)

XXX

After saying something insulting to me one day, I asked why she was so horrible to me. She smiled proudly. "You still come back for more, don't you?" It was then that I knew I needed to find a job far away from her so that I couldn't keep coming back.

Within a few months, I lived in Bognor Regis (a coastal town) and was working as a care assistant. I was almost entirely socially isolated, except for work, which I hated. Anxiety prevented me from doing anything other than work. I lived alone in a tiny rented bedsit. I had no friends, or partner, and limited contact with family members other than The Mother. Even though I lived further away, I was still drawn back to visit her (albeit less frequently).

On one visit, she told me the devastating news that my dog had died. Whilst belly laughing hysterically, she said she watched her die and did nothing to ease her suffering. I was dumbfounded by how much she enjoyed telling me the details……"She couldn't move, so she couldn't eat or drink for two days". I asked her what she did with her body. She refused to tell me. I assumed she threw her in the bin.

I couldn't think of this for a long time. I blocked it out. But, after having recovered from past traumas, I developed intrusive thoughts about the pain my dog must have suffered whilst she pottered around the house.

I became haunted by images of her going to bed knowing my dog was dying in the next room. I still haven't come to terms with this. It's what I find hardest to forgive. Because it's a peek into the truth of what she's capable of – when no one's looking.

My newfound clarity meant I had to process the guilt I felt for my naivety. It didn't occur to me that she could be capable of such cruelty to an innocent animal, despite how she'd treated me.

*Narcissists try to instil uncomfortable feelings in others. Feelings they struggle with. They also try to invalidate their victim by praising others for the same thing they ignore or discourage in their victim.*

## Chapter 41 - The narcissist flatters in order to gain control

For my 24th birthday, The Mother visited overnight. I got no card or present, but I felt pleased she'd come to see me. I wanted to go out for a meal, but she didn't want to, so we didn't mark the occasion in any way. I told her that I hated my life and I wanted to try to pursue my dreams again.

"Sure, you're a lovely care assistant. You're so caring! I can't imagine you doing anything else as good as you do this!"

She'd switched tactics. Rather than trying to gaslight me into believing how worthless and stupid I was, she took to flattery. She told me that I would be a fool to give it up. (This minimum wage job that I hated!)

When I told her that my mind was made up, that I would apply to University to study drama, she tried to convince me that I wasn't bright enough to do a degree. Failing would be an embarrassment. It would be better not to try, she said. She plead with me, trying to convince me that she was trying to save me from embarrassment. Secretly, I thought, 'I've tried to live life in a way that pleases you, but the payoff isn't worth it. Now, it's time to try things my way.'

What's most revealing about this time of my life is that I was at my most depressed (regularly self-harming now and frequently contemplating suicide); because of the life I was living. Yet her guidance was to continue to live the life I was living!

I didn't know that she had cruel intentions, but I had finally realised that her advice; any advice she gave, was not to be followed. This was a pivotal moment because despite how enmeshed I still was with her and how responsible I felt for her feelings, I had realised I was still feeling guilty about who and what I was. Guilt makes us people please. By acquiescing, by trying to please her, I gave her the power to wrap her claws around me even tighter. My attempts at placating her, and ingratiating myself, made her continue to over-involve herself in my life. I finally realised that there was no reward for my obedience. The more I tried to please her, the tighter the noose got around my neck. Instead of bringing about her love, I got embroiled in a strange, painful entanglement. I couldn't escape her, and yet I couldn't reach her. And yet, I continued to seek her approval.

XXX

I now had permanent scar tissue on both arms from years of self-harming. Within the next year, I would go on to attempt to kill myself twice more. I was what would be termed a 'functional depressive'. Carrying on life as normal in between bouts of self-destructive behaviour.

The toxic shame I was living with became increasingly debilitating. I felt embarrassed to exist. Not worthy enough to take up space on this earth. Yet, I got into drama school, Italia Conti, for a second time. But I couldn't go because Tony Blair had just scrapped discretionary grants. Luckily, I'd also applied to University, so I went there instead.

Despite being surrounded by others and living in halls, I felt very lonely. I could only connect with one person—an American exchange student who left after the first term. I couldn't connect with anyone else; try as I may. Uni was a very isolating experience that seemed to confirm my deepest fears about myself. Most of the students were a good six years younger than me. Most were from middle-class backgrounds. And most had supportive parents. I had nothing in common with these people.

The isolation I felt compounded the state of depression I was in. No one could know how ashamed I was to exist. It was just too embarrassing. It never occurred to me to go to a doctor, as I didn't think I had anything diagnosable. I just thought I was unworthy.

The obvious solution seemed to me to be suicide again. I decided after my fourth attempt that God must want me to endure the misery of life for some reason. So, I never tried again. Instead, I increasingly coped with my social anxiety, depression and loneliness by self-harming. Whenever I got the urge not to be here anymore, I'd cut. The release of blood provided an emotional release that was comforting, and the act of cutting allowed me to release tears that had been trapped inside me for years. And so, it became a ritualistic coping strategy that kept me from killing myself. An addictive habit that took years to break.

However, it also served to isolate me from others. I discovered that others felt uncomfortable when they saw my scars. People rarely mentioned it or asked questions, but I would feel people change towards me when they spotted a scar. Their reaction exacerbated my toxic shame. So, I isolated myself more and cut myself even more.

I still viewed my relationship with The Mother as important, and continued to believe that I could prove my worth to her by becoming successful. 'Then she'd love me', I said to myself. This was my firmly held view, despite evidence to the contrary.

XXX

Before going into the halls, I offered her the phone number. She refused. "It would be impossible to get hold of ye", she said. So, for the next three years, the relationship was maintained solely by me. Every Saturday, I'd put a £1 coin in the phone box to speak with her. I continued to live in denial and so hadn't picked up on the fact that she'd rather I didn't bother.

Oblivious to her disinterest in me, I went home to see her after the first term. I arrived at the house planning to spend Christmas with her, only to discover that she'd arranged a job interview for me for a job that would have me living miles away for the entire Christmas break!

I'd travelled on an overnight coach, so was in no condition to have an interview. But just like when I was 11 years old, she stopped me at the door before I even had a chance to take my coat off. I needed to leave the house immediately. Disoriented, I complied.

She'd arranged an interview for the position of a live-in care assistant in Guildford. Starting immediately. The woman I was assigned to was vile. After about a week, I was moved because she refused to feed me, despite food being included as part of my payment. The last straw came when she accused me of stealing her money. She raged at me publicly that she would report me for theft. Then found her £5 note. She mumbled a reluctant apology, but I knew I was done. After five days of hunger, I finally plucked up the courage to complain to the agency.

I had more freedom at the next house, but it was still an awful experience. If I thought I knew what isolation was – this was on a whole other level! I was allowed 1 hour a day to leave the house, but because it was so rural, there was nothing to do and nowhere to go. I was completely alone except for a doddery old lady who couldn't remember my name. My loneliness hit me particularly badly on Christmas Day. I walked out to a phone box to call a few people. No one answered. I broke down in the phone box. I didn't know how much more of this isolation I could take.

The following day, during my hour of freedom, I went out to the phone box to call the agency. I thought it might make me feel better to have some free time before returning to Uni. I was desperate for human contact, so I wanted to discuss the end of the contract. The woman said that because I'd left the other client early and didn't fulfil my 'three-week obligation per household, the contract started again' in the house I was now in. But my break from Uni was only two weeks. We had some heated words. I said I wasn't willing to stay on after the academic term started. I said I would be leaving to return to Uni on time, whether they had someone to replace me or not. (I wasn't usually so assertive, but I felt like I was going insane. And to jeopardise my degree for a job I hated was preposterous.) The woman defensively asked me why I took on the job when I had other obligations.

"Nobody explained to me at the interview that I'd be required to stay for three weeks," I said. "If I knew this, I would have turned the job down".

Did The Mother know?

Maybe she arranged the interview not just as a way of rejecting me but as a way of sabotaging my course as well?! Perhaps she was actively trying to prevent me from going back to Uni? I remained naïve to her intentions for a long time.

*'**Emotional thinking**' prevents a person from seeing the real motivations behind another's actions. (Being in a permanently mild state of disassociation prevented me from being able to connect the dots. However, I had a drive, a determination, and a passion that she could not extinguish.)*

# Chapter 42 - Awakening happens in stages

No matter what we do for the narcissist, no matter how much we give or give up, it will never be enough. We cannot fill the hole that's inside them.

I was aware of this much when I decided to go to University. But the power of psychological abuse is so strong that examples and proof can be right in front of our faces, and we still won't see it. Disassociation helped me survive my childhood, but it kept me enmeshed in the toxic relationship with her as an adult because I was utterly oblivious to the continuing abuse.

Although I still didn't have a word for it, my awareness of her withholding became more pronounced in my last year of Uni, simply because she made it so obvious.

I stayed with her for a term whilst directing a play with local school children as part of an elective. Towards the end of this time, I invited her to the performance. I foolishly thought she'd be proud of my work. The school was only a 30-minute walk from her house. The day of the performance was a nice day, and she had nothing better to do.

"It would be nice if you'd come. I'd appreciate it". I said whilst she sat with her back to me, refusing to engage. "Why won't you come?" I asked after some more silence. She turned the TV up. I said no more.

I went and enjoyed the performance alone. Although I got positive feedback from kids and teachers, sharing my achievement with someone would have been nice.

I returned home to silence. She asked nothing about the

performance, and I said nothing. Although I was now aware of her withholding, I didn't know why. Even though she'd spent the last two and a half years encouraging me to drop out; although she'd refused to attend any performance I was in; and even though she'd constantly downplayed and undermined my course to others, saying that I wasn't at an actual University, and I wasn't doing a real degree………..despite all this, I still couldn't see that she was envious, and was trying to sabotage my success. The fog was slowly starting to lift, though.

I had another significant realisation in my last year of Uni. I visited her the summer Uni ended. I was looking forward to seeing her because I'd lost a significant amount of weight. Despite how proud I was of my body, I was resigned to the fact that for me, being slimmer meant that I was almost always miserable, cold and hungry. But that didn't matter. I could squeeze into a size ten hot pants! Something that had been sitting in my wardrobe for years! I'd finally done it! She would be so proud of me, I thought. Her reaction would be worth the last few gruelling months of one meal a day.

My excitement evaporated almost immediately on seeing her, as she made no acknowledgement of my noticeable weight loss. I secretly fumed. I'd achieved what she'd wanted, finally! And I got no response whatsoever?! Her obsession with my body was a con! A smokescreen! It was just an excuse to criticise me! I'd been obsessing about this for the last 14 years because I thought it was the main reason she didn't love me. I now knew it was utterly irrelevant to how she felt about me.

I knew that if I'd come home a pound heavier, she would have noticed and said something. I knew she scrutinised my body to the nth degree, looking for things to criticise. So, I knew that it wasn't possible that she didn't notice I'd lost a stone (14lbs). I knew that she was deliberately withholding praise and acknowledgement from me. But, again, I didn't know why. Right then and there, I decided never to starve myself again.

XXX

A few months later, I plucked up the courage to address the issue with her. I never called her out on her behaviour; I just told her that I was done with dieting so I might get heavier, but I didn't care anymore. I wanted her to understand that I didn't want to hear what she thought of my body anymore.

"Whether it's positive or negative, I don't want to hear it." I reminded her that she'd been telling me I was overweight for 14 years, and still, she didn't feel that I'd succeeded in the weight loss she would have liked. Therefore, the obvious conclusion was that her nagging wasn't helpful, I said.

Surprisingly, she remained quiet. I suspect that she was gobsmacked. She didn't, of course, take any responsibility. Instead, she meekly defended her corner, denying that she'd ever said anything negative about my body! I was stunned into silence. I wasn't expecting her to lie so blatantly.

XXX

I found out a short time later from a family member that she told them she thought I was 'having a nervous breakdown' because of this conversation.

(She'd laid the groundwork for years for me to not be believed by others, saying that I was an attention seeker, lacking in common sense, and overly sensitive.) Now, because I'd dared to challenge her, the smear campaign got worse. I was no longer just a stupid, embarrassing failure; I was crazy too.

XXX

Due to our distorted perceptions, gaslighting, the trauma bond, and confidence issues, it takes years to untangle ourselves from the web the narcissist has weaved for us.

During this year, I had two significant realisations– 'She won't love me if I'm slimmer.' And 'she won't be proud of my successes.' This was my second most significant awakening after realising that I should no longer take advice from her.

*Most of us need a significant amount of therapy to achieve freedom from the narcissistic relationship. Matrix Reimprinting is the most successful trauma therapy I've found for recovering from narcissistic abuse.*

## Chapter 43 - From Lost Child to Golden Child

After 28 years of being The Lost Child, The Mother abruptly shifted gears. It was as if it suddenly dawned on her, six months before my graduation, that I might succeed! So, with no acknowledgement of this shift, she went from doing everything she could to sabotage my success to excitedly planning my graduation. I was annoyed that she'd invited herself but didn't dare say so.

After my degree, I planned to attend teacher training college. Despite inviting herself to my graduation, she still tried to dissuade me from continuing my education and training. When I asked her to clarify her problem with teaching as a career, she retorted, "it's' a job", as in, 'it's just a job', like having any minimum wage job. She smirked as she said it, seemingly aware of how ridiculous she sounded.

I asked, "Don't you want me to be happy?"

"Of course not", she replied, whilst holding my gaze and smirking. I was stunned into silence. Although I thought about this moment often, I never found the courage to mention it again.

XXX

It wasn't until I got my first teaching job and accompanying flat a year later that I briefly became the golden child. I think this change was strategic. No more, no less. If she'd continued with her rhetoric of how useless and stupid I was, despite the reality, she ran the risk of being exposed for the manipulative saboteur she is. It made more sense to engulf and control me whilst pretending to be 'only for (my) good'. She could continue to infantilise me by taking away all of my choices, and isolate me by demanding so much of my time that I had none left for others.

Underneath the surface, she still wanted to destroy me. She just changed strategy that's all. In the meantime, she became a parasite, enjoying my status and rewards as if they were hers.

XXX

Why would someone who's placed another in the role of being invisible suddenly start acting as if they notice them?

I believe for any narcissist, the answer is because they're suddenly getting positive narcissistic supply from their victim.

The Mother had given up calling me academically stupid by now, as reality had proved her wrong. Instead, she cleverly and subtly began to change the narrative, focussing more on 'common sense'. "That's book clever." She would say. "Book clever doesn't mean you're smart. There are many stupid educated people in the world. You need common sense to succeed in life".

It's a trait of narcissists to minimise the achievements of others. This is due to their grandiosity. Others' successes do not sit well with them because it challenges their distorted grandiose self-image. In The Mother's case, her grandiosity is secret because she is a covert narcissist.

I gradually realised that being the golden child wasn't what it was cracked up to be. It didn't feel like love. Instead, it felt like a slow strangulation of my soul. The enmeshment that came with that role was more detrimental to my mental health than being ignored for all those years. It felt like she wanted my life.

I had no say in the furniture or decorating of my new flat.

She made these choices as if they were hers. When I tried to make my own choices, she told me that I didn't know what I was talking about, and she did, so that's that. I didn't like her choices, but it didn't matter. She insisted on furnishing my flat with cheap second-hand mismatched items that looked like they should have been on the scrap heap. Now that I was earning good money, I wanted to get nice furniture that would last, but she forced me to buy such a cheap sofa that not even she could sit comfortably on it because it was so threadbare.

In hindsight, I realised that she was sabotaging me again. Trying to prevent me from having nice things because she didn't believe I deserved them. She even forced a chair on me that had been in her house the whole time I was alive, so it was at least 28 years old. She acted offended when I wanted to replace it a year later with a nice sofa. I wasn't allowed to throw out her decades-old cast-offs.

Despite her overbearing and engulfing behaviour, I perceived her desire to spend more time with me as good. I thought I was winning her over, and I was proud of what I'd achieved against all odds and thought she was too. So, I invited her for Christmas.

This turned out to be one of the biggest mistakes of my life. Not only did she outstay her welcome and violate my boundaries, but she also accepted my invitation with the sole purpose, I now believe, of turning me into an alcoholic. I'd never been much of a drinker. I didn't drink in my teens, and I didn't drink that much at Uni.

She'd always told me I would become an alcoholic like my father. And I'd be dead by age 40, just like my father. So, I stayed away from alcohol, scared that her prediction might come true.

I now understand that she was prophesying precisely what she wanted. In a sense, she was 'grooming' me, conditioning me to become exactly what she wanted me to be with reverse psychology. All this time, I thought she was making these forecasts out of fear. I don't believe that to be true anymore. When her prophesy didn't happen naturally, she nudged things along.

"How long are you planning on staying?" I asked when she arrived with multiple over-packed suitcases.

"Till you get sick of me," she replied, as she pushed past me into the hallway. Before making herself at home, she took out two bottles of wine and opened one. She then proceeded to drink every day she was with me. Drinking took away the 'walking on eggshells' feeling I always had around her. So, I joined in. I thought we were bonding.

During her stay, she displayed some strange behaviours, but not wanting to upset a guest in my home, and it being the first time I'd invited her for Christmas, I downplayed how annoyed I was. What I now understand to be 'enabling behaviour.'

One evening I noticed that she'd opened a present I'd bought for someone but hadn't gotten around to wrapping. She was halfway through the box of chocolates before I realised. She did act sorry when I said it was someone's present, but then she carried on eating the chocolates and didn't offer to replace the box.

Another time during her stay, I realised a picture had disappeared from my bedroom wall. It was an erotic picture. Not offensive, not pornographic, just slightly erotic.... arty. I asked her where it went. She tried to convince me that she didn't know what I was talking about. I decided it had somehow fallen off the wall and got lodged somewhere because I wanted to believe her.

I was confronted with the truth the day I moved out. Facing an empty flat, I had to admit that she'd gotten rid of the picture. She must have thrown it down the chute while my back was turned.

I didn't understand that these were flagrant violations of my boundaries. I didn't understand how disrespectful she was. And I didn't understand the latter to be 'crazy-making', gaslighting behaviour.

Come New Year's Eve, she was still with me, so I had to cancel my plans discreetly. Again, I was annoyed but said nothing. She didn't leave my flat until I started to initiate the drinking. Her work was done.

After she left, I started to drink alone in my flat on Friday evenings. I'd just moved to the area, so I had no friends locally, and my job kept me too busy to find time for relationships. So, it was the easiest way of relaxing, opening a bottle of wine on a Friday night.

Being an introvert, teaching exhausted me. I had no desire to go out and mix with people, after being around people all day, all week. I needed my alone time, so wine became a source of comfort. It wasn't long before I started drinking every evening after school.

During this golden child phase, we'd fallen into the dynamic of me fawning over her. I'd treat her to the theatre and restaurants almost weekly. Having no friends meant she had all my free time.

Despite doing everything I could to please her, she seemed to want to hurt me. Narcissists are wired to be perpetually disappointed and easily irritated, even by fawning. The irony is that although narcissists demand admiration and attention, when they get it, they often reject it. Especially if they're covert. They're disgusted by our pathetic attempts to please them, so feel justified in amping up their contemptuous unreasonable behaviour. How dare we try to please them?!
I started noticing that no matter how hard I tried to make things work with us, she started to distance herself from me.

Riverdance was a big thing at the time. I asked her to see it with me repeatedly. Being Irish, I thought she'd appreciate it. But she turned her nose up like it wasn't her thing. Then, the night of the last sell-out show at our local theatre, she spontaneously offered the information that she'd gone to see the show with her friend. I was angry, hurt, and confused. I asked her why she'd refused to see it with me. She tried to gaslight me again, "I didn't think you'd enjoy it!" She wanted me to know, in a passive-aggressive way that made her unaccountable; that it was me she was rejecting, not the show.

XXX

I didn't know it then, but narcissists are bored by any conversation that doesn't revolve around them. One day I was telling her a story about something or other on the phone. I don't remember the content, but it was a positive story. I was in a good mood. Suddenly, the line went dead. She'd put the phone down whilst I was speaking. I was so furious that I called her right back. Incredulous, I asked, "What was that?"

She said that she hung up because there was an awkward silence. I corrected her. "No, there wasn't. I was in the middle of speaking, and you hung up on me!" I ended the call because, as Dr Ramani on YouTube says, the conversation was a dead end.

When she did grace me with her presence, her entitlement never allowed her to express gratitude for the gifts I bought. Her reaction to a facial I'd paid for one Mother's Day was particularly painful and embarrassing. After a meal in a restaurant, I excitedly said I had a surprise for her and walked her to a salon where I'd booked for us to have facials together.

During mine, I could hear her in the next room, repeatedly saying to her facialist, "How long is this gonna take? What you doing that for? Hurry up, then! Is it over yet?" I silently cringed throughout.

When we left the salon, neither of us mentioned her behaviour or the facial. I just made a silent note never to do anything like that for her again.

I gradually started to resent my efforts, and started retracting the special treatment she'd grown accustomed to. This led to a battle of wills.

The next time we met in a pub in Central London, I didn't take charge like I usually did. Instead, I sat at the table with her. Curious to see how long it would take for her to put her hand in her pocket. It was a tense moment, as I tried to resist the urge to take out my purse. We sat……and sat…….. and sat. Then The Mother said she didn't like this pub. It was too noisy. So, we went to another pub.

I sat at a table again, making no offer to buy drinks. She got up in a huff, saying that the pub was too smoky.

We went to a third pub. She again left after a few minutes, saying that the menu didn't look good. By this point, I started to fume silently, and planned on going home if she was to walk out of a fourth pub.

I didn't need to say anything. She found the fourth pub suitable, just; and finally went to the bar. She came back with just her drink, though. Not mine. I didn't mind. It was progress. I walked to the bar to get my drink feeling triumphant. The Mother 0. Charlie 1.

### XXX

I found out later that whilst she was drinking with me every weekend, she was telling everyone what an alcoholic I was. Now that I was a drinker, she could resume being a self-sacrificing martyr—her most accomplished role to date.

After one of her 'concerned' visits, I went into my kitchen to see that she'd dug out all the empty bottles from the bin and lined them up on the countertop with a note, pointing out how much money the bottles had cost me.

If looking at this act in isolation, it could be argued that it come from tough love. But looking at any act in isolation distorts the facts.

Aside from causing my dog unnecessary suffering in her last days, bringing alcohol into my life was probably one of her most nefarious acts because alcohol is so destructive if it gets a hold of you, as it did me.

### XXX

Only a year later did I realise I had a problem. I was standing at a shop checking out. Suddenly, a horrible shaky, sweaty feeling came over me. I didn't know at the time, but it was withdrawal symptoms. As I looked up at the clock, I thought, 'I could fancy a drink'. It was 11.15 am. The feeling I had at that moment is one I will never forget. I was horrified, scared, and ashamed. I thought, 'I'm in trouble'.

In the previous months of daily drinking, I told myself I wasn't an alcoholic because I could choose to stop if I wanted to. I just didn't want to.

I'd also made up a rule that justified and minimised my drinking. I theorised that drinking from midday was acceptable (when not working.) Drinking before midday was for alcoholics. And now, here I was, craving a drink before noon.

Excessive alcohol use whilst being in an almost permanent state of disassociation made me even more mentally fragile over time, making me more vulnerable and susceptible to further gaslighting, until I thought I was having some sort of mental breakdown. Before the year was out, I was suicidal again. I thought, 'we can't both live my life, so if she wants my life, she can have it'. Even these feelings she tried to control. She busied herself with organising a doctor's appointment for me, and involved herself in ensuring I took my anti-depressants. I wanted to scream, as she shoved the pills into my hand, 'you're the problem!' but I had no energy left to fight. I was an emotionally exhausted cardboard cut-out, going through the motions of life, but not living.

*Much research suggests a strong link between addiction and childhood trauma. The **National Institute of Health (NIH)** 'reports that those who sustain childhood trauma are at extremely high risk for developing alcohol addiction. And yet, this already well-established knowledge is not reflected in funded addiction services or the NHS, (at least in front line/primary care services.)**

# Chapter 44 - Repetition Compulsion

Narcissistic parents can only operate in the extremes of ignoring and engulfing. I interpreted her engulfing of me as an attempt at love or care on some level. However, I knew that what I was experiencing wasn't love. It was too uncomfortable to be love; but with withholding being my only other option, (because those are the extremes she operates within); I tolerated her bizarre enmeshing behaviour.

This polarisation, along with occasional breadcrumbing, causes the victim to become addicted. And so the trauma bond is created.

XXX

Despite my depression, I finally succeeded in my dream of attending Drama school at 31 years old. I was accepted on the same day as the audition, on The Mother's birthday. The drama school was closer to her place than mine, so, I decided to kill two birds with one stone. On my way home from the audition, I popped into hers' to give her a birthday present, which she did not react to. I also told her that I had gotten into drama school. To which she also did not react.

I pre-empted her withholding by relaying the news as deadpan as possible. Then felt a pang of sadness, that I couldn't express my excitement, or expect her to be excited for me.

XXX

For some time now, she'd been single again and dating

casually. She'd made it clear that she didn't want me interacting with these men because I looked gay, apparently. She had this theory that if a boyfriend saw me, on first sight, he'd immediately know I was gay, and would somehow deduce that she must also be gay! So, I avoided getting to know her boyfriend out of respect for her.

During my visit, the day of the audition, her doorbell rang unexpectedly. Suddenly she looked like she'd shit her pants! "Oh my God!! He's here!! You have to go! He can't see you!" (Talk about role reversal!) I calmly explained that there was only one way out of her house, so I would have to go past her new boyfriend.

"Just go quickly then", she whined. We walked to the door together, and she opened it. Pleasantries followed.

"Hello. Nice to meet you. I'll be going now." I smiled and waved as I said goodbye. He suggested I stay for tea.

"No. I must be getting back. It's late. Thanks for the offer, though. Take care. Bye."

A few days later, she phoned me to scold me for being rude. "You could have at least spent some time talking to him! He thought you were so rude walking out like that. I was very embarrassed!" She used him to manipulate me into feeling guilty, even though I did exactly as she'd asked.

XXX

I was accepted into drama school in West London. I lived in East London, so, staying with her during the week made both practical and financial sense. Months before, I'd asked her if I could stay, and she said 'yes'. So, I took 'yes' to mean 'yes'. Why would it mean anything else, right?

Naively, I didn't think things would be too difficult between us. I'd be out of the house from early morning, until 7.30 pm/8 pm. So, we wouldn't need to interact with each other that much.

Regardless, within a month, things had become unbearably awkward. There was a silent tension that grew every day. She treated me like a stranger, never acknowledging my presence.

Things were so awkward I felt compelled to address it. One day, as I bumped into her on the top landing, I did. She was about to walk down the stairs when I stopped her to say, "Mum, can we talk? Why is this so awkward?"

She grabbed the bannister and started swaying back and forth, clutching her heart, saying "My heart! My heart! I can't take it! You're going to kill me!"

I decided my only option was to leave without saying anything. I chose to gather up all my belongings and leave when she was out. Awkwardly, she happened to return as I was leaving with the last of my things. Her face said she was registering that I was leaving for good, but neither of us acknowledged the fact.

So, I returned to my flat, deciding that the four-hour daily commute and £35pw travel expenses were a better option than staying with her. We never mentioned why I left.

XXX

I suppose because I'd already had several months of counselling, I saw the situation for what it was. I knew she didn't want to take responsibility for wanting me to leave. I also knew that the tension between us couldn't be explained away by blaming myself for being oversensitive or paranoid.

XXX

Lyndsay C. Gibson explains why conversations with people like The Mother are so difficult. 'They stick to a well-worn script to avoid dangerous emotional intimacy.'

It finally worked. I started to withdraw quietly, and stopped seeing her in person. Instead, I began to use my time and money on therapy.

XXX

The Mother was a more powerful addiction than my issues with food and alcohol. Longer lasting and much more toxic. The world of psychology and recovery would say that my behaviours with her were based around 'repetition compulsion.'

*'**Repetition Compulsion'** - An attempt to fix a problem by doing the same thing repeatedly, hoping for a different outcome. Fun fact....... repetition compulsion is also the definition of insanity!*

## Chapter 45 - The road to recovery

During the period of engulfment, before drama school, the more time I spent with her, the more I had to face the painful truth that any time I spent with her was distressing. I was quite frankly either chronically bored or anxious around her. She wasn't interested in anything other than herself, so conversation was always strained.

It was only after repeated efforts at dialogue and trying to find different approaches, all of which failed, that I began to see how uncompromising she was. I eventually became so frustrated, hurt and angry, that I took the only avenue I could see when I returned to living in my flat full time. I gradually lessened my phone calls to her.

Our interactions became more difficult the older I got. Partly because I was becoming more awakened to the truth and perhaps also because she felt more and more challenged by me. The catalyst for withdrawing from her came one summer afternoon.

I fainted at the bank; then an ambulance took me to the hospital, where I was given the all-clear. Travelling home on the bus alone later that day, I had a realisation. I had no one to tell. If it had been something serious, no one would have cared. Suddenly, I felt very lonely.

Even though I'd been spending a lot of time with her up to this point, I didn't feel I could tell her because I knew she wouldn't be interested.

Before reading self-help books, I would've ignored my feelings and called her anyway, and she'd be disinterested, and I'd inevitably be hurt. (Repetition Compulsion).

This time, I didn't call her. This was my first tiny step to freedom. I remembered the self-help advice I'd read – that we can't spend our lives waiting for others to change. We have to change, and the other person will follow.

Based on this advice, I gradually stopped creating interactions with her that hurt me. For the first time, I dared to put my painful suspicion about our relationship to the test. How would I ever know if she wanted a relationship with me if I always did all the work? I'd been calling her every Saturday without fail for the last five years. How could she reciprocate if I never gave her the space to?

In an attempt to get to the truth, I didn't call her that Saturday. It was a difficult day, full of the withdrawal symptoms of guilt, fear and delusion. I was convinced she'd be angry that I hadn't called and feared an aggressive phone call from her, out of habit, if nothing else.

Sunday morning, I told myself, 'she must have had a busy day yesterday'. I was still 100% convinced I'd hear from her by Sunday night. I still feared she would be angry or hurt by the missed phone call.

But the weekend turned into a week, and a week turned into a month. I was devastated. My feelings had been right all along. If I didn't make the relationship happen, it didn't happen. The reality that she didn't care about me was a bitter pill to swallow after all my efforts with her.

Fainting in the bank made me realise that if something serious ever happened to me, she would just go about her business, never thinking to check on me. It was the most painful realisation I'd ever had, and it was also scary, particularly because I lived alone and was socially isolated.

Zoe from 'Live Abuse Free' on YouTube states that we need to not need anything from a person in order to be able to see them for who they are. This is 'Rational thinking' as opposed to 'Emotional Thinking'. If we need someone to be something to meet our needs, it clouds our perception of them. Of course, it's obvious now. The clues were there all along. But, because of my 'emotional thinking', I couldn't see them.

### XXX

I thought back to the Christmas before I'd invited her to mine. At the time, I vowed it would be the last Christmas I'd spend with her because she made it so miserable. It was only her and I. She came in to the lounge, where I was sitting, and accused me of breaking her freezer. I said I hadn't touched it. She insisted that I was lying. "The freezer was working, and now, it isn't." She continued to insist that I was the culprit.

I was so angry that I couldn't speak to her, so naturally, things were frosty between us. Then she suddenly decided that she was now the victim of my behaviour. She said that if I was going to spoil Christmas Day by sulking, I might as well go home. She knew full well there was no way for me to get home. There was no public transport, and a cab would have cost a fortune. So, I had to sit it out until the first available bus, days later. It was awful. She didn't seem to have many people in her life other than me, but she still couldn't help picking fights with me.

### XXX

With the help of counselling and self-help books, I gradually started to change our dynamic simply by refusing to be manipulated by her. The silent treatment didn't have the same effect on me anymore. It still hurt, but I knew that the answer wasn't to jump through her hoops.

The battle of wills continued. Her silent treatment lasted for longer and longer. Months turned into years simply because I wasn't making the efforts I used to.

She made a huge error in giving me such extended periods of the silent treatment. I began to realise that it was a blessing, not a curse. Without her in my life, I began to feel free. As the fog lifted, I started to see things more clearly.

Therapy started the process of remembering some traumatic

events that I had long since 'forgotten'. It also helped to unlock the trauma of other events that I did remember, but only in a fragmented way.

### XXX

Over the next 17 years, I would understand that not remembering is our subconscious self's/inner child's way of protecting us from what we're not ready to process.

Some experts in the field believe that narcissists are often empty inside. Empaths who spend enough time with narcissists may feel their hollowness and mistakenly think the feeling is theirs. In all likelihood, it's not. For anyone who's never experienced this hollowness, it's like boredom, but a terrifying existential one.

### XXX

We went' low contact' from the Saturday I didn't call her. If I'd had the courage, we might have gone 'no contact' cold turkey since she continued to make no effort. But I didn't have the courage, and I was still scared of upsetting her.

So, I continued to call her on significant days such as her birthday, Mother's Day and Christmas Day. I've since understood this as 'reverse hoovering'. (Her belief that her withholding would be so unbearable for me that I'd hoover myself back in, which is what I was doing.) I continued to try to maintain and improve the relationship, despite The Mother being increasingly hostile every time I phoned.

### XXX

That's all it took for our relationship to deteriorate beyond the point of repair. That one moment. That one decision, to not call her that Saturday. That's how fragile our relationship had been all along. And yet, I still believed that I could make reconciliation happen between us. This delusion was fed by lots of pseudo-spiritual guidance and self-proclaimed self-help gurus. I wasted many years and much effort because of one lie I was repeatedly told – that we have the power to transform anything if we want to.

We may have the power to transform many things, but making a narcissist love us, isn't one of them. Author Lyndsey C Gibson calls this hope we maintain, no matter what, our 'healing fantasy'. (Fantasies we create to get through the unbearable reality of our life.) My belief in her underlying authenticity kept me hooked and under her control for 38 years.

*The healing process must start from a place of self-compassion. This is the first step towards healing. Reducing contact with her, was my first act of self-compassion.*

## Chapter 46 - Life changing epiphanies

I took the first step towards my self-help journey in my mid-20s when I came across a book called 'The Assertive Woman' by Stanlee Phelps and Nancy K. Austin. A friend lent it to me after I saw it on her bookshelf. Shortly into the book, I realised that I couldn't even begin to try the exercises it suggested because I had a deep-seated belief that I didn't have a right to assert myself. Something inside me knew there was something 'off' with this belief. After all, I believed everyone else had the right to assert themselves. And so, I realised at the time that I needed to work on this self-sabotaging belief. I just didn't know how.

It would be at least four years before I'd start counselling. The catalyst for this was flashbacks from the abuse I'd suffered at gymnastics. The first one took me completely by surprise whilst I was out running.

I spent the next eight months crying profusely at every session. The counsellor made me feel validated, which helped me to develop a stronger sense of self. She was the only person who said, 'I think your mum has a personality disorder.' However, I was dismissive, so she never mentioned it again.

I'd never heard of the term 'personality disorder'. I didn't know what the term meant. But I jumped to The Mother's defence and insisted the issue was me. I was blind to the irony that all I ever spoke and cried about during these sessions was how she treated me.

The awareness I'd always had of her enduring disappointment and disinterest in my existence developed throughout my 20s and 30s into a more conscious and painful realisation that I could no longer ignore.

I did a lot of reflecting during these years. Without her constant gaslighting, I could finally put the jigsaw pieces together and make sense of her nonsensical behaviour. Epiphany after epiphany followed.

'So, she tells me I'm stupid and a failure, not because she believes it to be so, but because she wants me to believe it to be so! She wanted me to give up! She wanted me to fail! So that she could be proved right! So that she could feel justified in her disappointment of me!'

I finally got it! Her frustration towards me was because I'd proved her wrong, despite her sabotage and my low self-worth. Over and over again.

I was still to be misled by a few red herrings, though. After a few months of silent tension, she initiated contact, inviting me to dinner with her and an uncle. I childishly believed this invitation to be an olive branch, and I rationalised that she needed the excuse of my uncle's presence to break the ice. I accepted the invitation, feeling this was a breakthrough.

On my arrival at her house, she seemed tearful. I thought she'd reflected on things. I was hopeful that this was the beginning of a more reciprocal relationship. During dinner, I did a lot of the talking, pretending there was no tension between us. He'd no idea that we hadn't spoken in nearly a year.

Little did I know, she'd invited me to protect her image. I was there to convince him that things were fine between us because that's what she cares about, what others think of her.

Now, I saw the truth; I couldn't un-see it. For almost my entire life, I've believed The Mother to be dumb as a rock. Now I think she is a master manipulator who wears stupidity and ignorance as a mask.

She only ever invited me to hers one more time after that, for Christmas dinner. I asked her who else was going to be there.

(After being blamed for breaking her freezer a few Christmases ago, I wasn't going to risk being alone with her again.) She said that her boyfriend would be there.

Suddenly it dawned on me that this was the uncle situation repeating itself. She invited me for Christmas to give her boyfriend the impression that we got on.

I was insulted that she thought I'd fall for this twice. Also, the fact that she called on Christmas Eve annoyed me, which is historical behaviour for her. Her children get last-minute invites because she hangs out for better offers.

I declined because I could no longer stand the façade. I chose to spend Christmas alone instead. This made her angry. "What am I supposed to say to (latest boyfriend)"?! I suggested that she could tell him the truth. There's a novel idea! Or not tell him the truth. The choice was hers.

She didn't try to pretend that she was concerned, upset or even curious about why I'd rather be alone on Christmas Day than be with her. She was angry that she couldn't control or manipulate me anymore.

XXX

My next phase of growth happened after dating a narcissist. I didn't know that was what she was at the time, but I knew that she faked emotions. For whatever reason, I could see through her behaviour more easily than I could see through The Mothers.

One red flag was her tendency to create situations she could rescue me from. For example, I'd shared with her that I'd appreciate a heads-up before entering a social situation because of my anxiety, as I didn't like surprises. She didn't do what I asked, claiming she'd forgotten.

The next time the situation arose, I saw her looking out a window, watching a large group of her friends coming down a walkway. Her friends that she'd invited, without telling me in advance, again. She held my hands, saying, "Oh, no! I forgot to tell you again! Are you ok?"

On the surface, it seemed like she was trying to comfort me. But I could sense that her 'concern' was hollow. She'd created the situation so that she could act like my rescuer. My instinct was to not give her that satisfaction. So I acted cool, calm and collected.

I watched her behaviour more closely, and saw some similarities with The Mother. For example, she'd pick illogical fights. Like the time we'd visited her hometown of Manchester. She took me to a very upmarket bar. I was more used to gay Soho, so the luxury of this bar impressed me. I remember that there was a lot of marble. It looked very moneyed. I scanned the room, impressed, "Wow! This is nice!" A two-hour argument followed in which she accused me of presuming Manchester to be a shit hole!

How she broke up with me also felt like she was playing with my emotions. One minute we were walking down the street, holding hands, looking in an estate agent's window, and discussing moving in together. Fifteen minutes later, we were in a restaurant when she said, "I don't think this is working". I was hurt and confused but civilised about it. She wanted to stay and order the meal. I suddenly had no appetite. So, we left our drinks and walked to the train station.

Then she suggested coming back to mine. I said I wasn't trying to be a bitch, but if she wanted to return to my flat, she'd be sleeping on the sofa. She seemed offended, wanting to return to my flat and sleep in my bed. After dumping me

Later, she told me that she'd dumped me because she didn't think I could look after her when she was ill. (She'd had a minor accident on her bike earlier in the week. No hospital treatment was required. There were no scars, and no damage to the bike. It was more of a shock than anything). That night I cooked dinner, did the washing up and tidied up. I thought I was looking after her.

It seems she'd held a grudge that I hadn't answered my phone immediately on the day of the accident. (I was at Drama School, where they were very strict about using mobile phones. We weren't allowed to have them on us at any point in the day during lessons.)

As it was coming to our final end-of-year performance, I was busy rehearsing through breaks, so I didn't get her message until the end of the day. Even after explaining all of this to her, she still dumped me for not answering the phone quickly enough. She used this as evidence that I wouldn't be kind and nurturing if she were sick.

Even though I knew she was being unreasonable, I set about jumping through hoops to prove to her, as a friend now, that I can take care of someone when they're sick. Suddenly she seemed to be 'sick' a lot.

The straw that broke the camel's back came when she phoned at 3 am, expecting me to get on a night bus to an all-night shop five minutes from her flat, so I could deliver her some jelly babies! She couldn't go because she had 'the flu'. I said 'no' and stopped bothering to prove that I was a good caretaker.

I happened to be with her the day I bought a life-changing book. 'The Mythology of Self-Worth', by Richard L Franklin. It helped me become conscious of the 'Vicious Inner Critic' by working on the book's CBT (Cognitive Behavioural Therapy) exercises. One day she said, "I don't like how that book is changing you". I chuckled to myself.

There's a part of the book where the author states that 'when you start to change, some people will find it very difficult. They may even discourage you from reading this book!' I felt enlightened and empowered, and I didn't care if she didn't like me anymore.

XXX

I started to notice that other people in my life were equally disrespectful and manipulative. I met up with some friends in Central London to celebrate one birthday, and I suggested we eat at Pizza Hut. Half the group decided to go to a Steak House instead, despite knowing I was a vegetarian.

They left, and I didn't see them for the rest of the evening. I was so cut off from my feelings that it didn't occur to me that they weren't being very nice to me. None of the Steak House crowd acknowledged that it was my birthday. I got no card or present, but this went unnoticed by me. I was completely oblivious to how little they valued me.

Shortly afterwards, I met up with one of them for a drink. It was clear by the time we sat down that the purpose of this meeting was to tell me off. She felt the need to address how 'disappointed' she was that I hadn't accompanied her and the others to the Steak House. 'Especially as' they 'had bothered to come out to celebrate' my 'birthday'. She thought I should have complied with their wishes, and celebrated my birthday where they wanted to—classic entitlement and projection. The worst bit of all this is that it still didn't resonate with me how unreasonable she was being. I apologised.

XXX

In some ways, the following year was quite lonely because I was finally brave enough to stop bothering with friends that weren't friends at all. I now accepted the harsh truth. That they tolerated me because I allowed them to mistreat me.

As soon as I pushed back, there was radio silence, just like with The Mother. I imagined there would be some kind of conflict, but asserting my boundaries was easier than that. They all retreated when they saw that I wasn't so easy to push around.

Since I was now utterly alone in the world, I had nothing to do but work on myself. Which was all I did for about a year. There was freedom in accepting the truth. I was no longer living with cognitive dissonance. My words and actions could now finally align with how I felt.

I could be me.

*If a narcissist has raised us, it's more than likely, we will attract other narcissists into our life because we've already been conditioned to accept their unacceptable behaviour.*

# Chapter 47 - Courage repels narcissists

For the next five years, The Mother barely spoke to me. I stood my ground though. Determining that I would interact with her on my terms, not hers. I needed that time to build my courage, in order to attempt an honest conversation with her. That strength came from finding love.

XXX

I met my ex-wife on a Saturday evening nearly 16 years ago, after getting a text from a 'fair-weather' friend asking me to come out. I almost didn't. It was late and cold, and she was all the way across the other side of London. But, after some contemplation, I half-heartedly went.

I walked into a group of pretty inebriated people, stone-cold sober. A lady sitting with her back to me, turned around and locked eyes with me. She smiled, patted the chair beside her, saying "Come sit here."

Immediately I felt safe around her. She exuded energy I'd never encountered before. I was intrigued. Her eyes showed me that she was kind, sincere, compassionate, and loyal.

I 100% believe that because of the work I'd done on myself the year before, I finally attracted someone on the vibration of love. I was still struggling and living in a lot of fear. I still had lots of work to do, but my energy had shifted enough to attract this significant change. This then changed the course of the rest of my life.

Navigating my way through this relationship was still

complicated. It was a steep learning curve because it was unfamiliar territory for me. I had to learn to have honest conversations, and I had to learn not to project fears and anxieties created by The Mother, onto her.

This was the most significant leap in my recovery; someone finally seeing and accepting me for who I was. I now had an ally with which to face the world.

The Mother still tried to sabotage my happiness. Despite our strained relationship, she still felt compelled to try to manipulate and control me. For example, over the years, I'd repeatedly tried to explain to her how intolerable my flat and area had become. (I'd moved there blindly, with the promise of a cheap council flat that went with my first teaching job.) It was ok for a couple of years, but then a drug den started operating in my building, and all hell broke loose. Gangs roamed the streets; bus drivers refused to stop down my street because gangs would 'rush' the bus, terrorising the passengers; the neighbours played music all night long, and nobody could stop them. I couldn't even jog or cycle anymore because of harassment and complaining to the council was pointless.

Whenever I tried to tell her how unsafe I felt and how unhappy I was there, during our sporadic conversations, she'd minimise things, telling me how great the flat was and that I'd be 'foolish to let it go.'

The breaking point came when I arrived back at my flat after spending a weekend away and saw a wooden cross on the grass just outside my front door. A 36-year-old man had been beaten to death.

Nobody could convince me that I was 'making a mountain out of a molehill' anymore. It was clear evidence that I was not safe. Even after I told her this, she still wasn't moveable. She continued with the same rhetoric. She did everything she could to convince me to stay where I was unhappy and unsafe. However, she could no longer gaslight me. (I made it clear that no matter what she thought, I would move with my girlfriend Predencia, (who eventually became my wife) to the seaside.

She tried to enlist a sister as a flying monkey. To her, she portrayed my moving as a silly childish fantasy. She laughed at my dream to live in a safe area as if I 'had ideas above my station'.

After I moved, she became notably frostier. She couldn't hide her irritation that I was happy. I could now see these links. The happier and more independent I became, the angrier she became.

I didn't understand the gravity of this realisation, though. Naively, I was slightly amused. It was apparent now that she was childish, and it was evident that she was envious of my relationship. But I thought she would eventually come around if I handled her with kid gloves. I believed that things would be fine once she got to know Predencia. I was still deluded enough to think she wanted me to be happy underneath the childish envy.

XXX

Shortly after Predencia and I met, I had my last 1-2-1 meeting with her. At the time I didn't know it would be the last. If I had, I might have been even braver than I was!

I went to meet her to have an honest conversation. Hoping this would improve our relationship. How naive! She seemed to sense a shift in my energy.

Following the advice from self-help books, I decided to be direct. I expected that things would magically get better between us just by being transparent.

"You weren't very emotionally supportive", I bravely challenged. Hoping this would become the deep and meaningful conversation I'd longed for my whole life. She threw back at me defensively that she'd occasionally lent me money. (With high interest. I found out later I could've got a cheaper deal from the bank).

I didn't let her derail the conversation. Instead, I tried to get her to see the connection between her behaviours of the past and my reactions.

I asked her to remember when she used to force me to date men. I reminded her of when she'd said, "Why don't you marry a man and do what you want on weekends?" I finally asked what I'd wanted to do a long time ago. "Was this man I'd marry, for you, supposed to know? To be in on the lie? Or was I supposed to con someone for you?"

She looked at me blankly. Clearly, this hypothetical man was as irrelevant as he was needed. At least his feelings were irrelevant. If he was hurt and betrayed, it didn't matter. If I lived a miserable life in a loveless marriage, it didn't matter. All that mattered was that I reflected well on her. I told her that her lack of acceptance made me suicidal. She responded that my suicide attempts were a 'cry for help.' I didn't dare to ask, 'then why didn't you help me?' Eventually, she started crying.

I was aware on some level that her tears were a manipulation tactic, and I was level-headed enough to know that I'd said nothing to warrant the meltdown I saw before me. I knew she was deflecting and trying to make me feel guilty. And I did feel somewhat guilty. Seeing this formidable woman I'd been scared of my whole life crumble so easily wasn't nice. It was uncomfortable and a little embarrassing.

XXX

Life Coach Lisa A. Romano has a YouTube video called 'Narcissists destroy boundaries - They can't and won't accept them'. This video helped me to understand the theory behind why this was the last time we ever met alone.

She wasn't going to allow me to assert a boundary simply because she didn't care. It was always her way or the highway. It was always written into the script that if I ever tried to assert myself or if I ever tried to think about my needs, that would be the end.

Subconsciously I always knew this. But because she'd done such a good job convincing me that everything was my fault,

I believed I could fix things. Even though every time I tried to assert a boundary, things got worse between us. Still, I hoped she would soon soften and understand that I meant no harm by being honest.

She refused to speak to me for two years. She couldn't forgive me for calling her 'emotionally unsupportive,' telling other family members how much I'd hurt her.

I called her every week initially, hoping to smooth things over, but eventually, I gave up. I could see that she wasn't softening.

*Narcissists will let a relationship deteriorate for the slightest reason. They are almost impossible to make up with. Unlike with others, honesty destroys a relationship with a narcissist. It's intolerable to them*.

# Chapter 48 - Special Occasions

Things were changing. I was changing. I was no longer willing to accept her breadcrumbs, and I certainly wasn't willing to take the blame when I knew I'd done nothing wrong.

That Christmas, I was surprised to get a card from her. In fact I was over the moon when I saw her handwriting. Thinking this was the step forward I'd wanted from her my whole life. I thought she'd demonstrated some maturity.

"You see!" I said to Predencia, "I knew she'd get over it. She just needed some time." I opened the card and immediately felt like I'd been punched in the face.

'I'm spending Christmas in Spain – alone because I can't bear to be in the same country as you.' It immediately triggered an emotional flashback. I took on the guilt and shame she wanted me to feel. At that moment, I felt that I deserved to be punished for how I'd hurt her. I regretted my horrible mistake, fearing that she'd never forgive me. 'If I could go back in time, I wouldn't have said what I did,' I thought. Still not realising how vengeful and manipulative she is.

After some more time, I could see her motivation. I knew what she wrote made no sense. We'd hardly spoken in years, so how would being in the same country as me on Christmas Day affect her? It wouldn't! I finally realised that she was just trying to hurt me.

XXX

Over the next few years, we would meet occasionally, but never alone. The next time our paths crossed was at a family wedding. Whilst we stood together for the photographer, she patted my hips, saying, "keeping the weight off, aren't ye"? It took a while for Predencia to understand that it wasn't a compliment. The implication was that she was still judging my worth according to my weight. Even though we weren't in each other's lives, she wanted me to still obsess about my weight because it mattered to her.

She didn't seem hostile, however. I thought this was progress. So, I invited her for dinner in London so she could meet Predencia properly. She invited along my sister, which I didn't mind, but then she started to triangulate, making arrangements only through her, which I did mind. I had visions of us all sitting at a table, with her saying, 'daughter, can you tell another daughter to pass the salt, please!' She would only call and speak to me once I'd threatened to cancel the meeting.

We met on a bitterly cold Sunday afternoon in Trafalgar Square. After a Chinese, we went to a pub, where she became uncharacteristically affectionate towards me, stroking my hair and rubbing my back. I accepted all this unprecedented affection gratefully, without question. I soaked it all up like a sponge. I had no idea why she was so affectionate, but I didn't want her to stop.

Only now, with the benefit of hindsight, can I understand that she wanted to make a good impression on Predencia. If she'd believed The Mother's very convincing display of love and affection, it would cast doubt on my story. She was setting me up to look like a liar in front of my partner.

If this plan failed, which it did, she could at least enjoy making my sister jealous. She barely acknowledged her presence, even though she'd used her for a lift, and begged her to stay 'for support', saying that she was scared Predencia would 'drag her down an alleyway and beat (her) up!'

She may have been a little scared that I might have told Predencia everything, and perhaps expected that she would be protective of me or even angry at her.

Either that, or playing the victim was a manipulative way of ensuring she got a lift home. Having my sister present was all about her own needs being met, but instead of being nice to her, the person who'd chauffeured her there and doubled as her bodyguard; she ignored her—focussing all her attention on me.

I didn't know what she said about Predencia until years later, so in my innocence, I believed that the meal went well. So, I invited her to my home for Mother's Day dinner. Again, my sister drove her.

She was pleasant enough, but made a negative impression on Predencia this time by monologuing about how her achievements. Predencia was more interested in hearing stories about me when I was younger. "Where were the kids?" She asked, trying to redirect the conversation.

"They were there." She waved her hand dismissively and carried on bragging about her achievements. This was the last Mother's Day I ever celebrated with her.

XXX

Narcissists can be nosy due to their envy and competitive nature. Nothing means anything unless it can be compared favourably against someone else. This was why she so readily agreed to come to my home. Once she'd satisfied her curiosity, she made no more attempts to visit me. I believe now that the fact that I was happy and doing well for myself made her so angry that she wanted nothing more to do with me. But of course, being a covert, she couldn't be honest about it. Instead, she became increasingly difficult. Being either overtly aggressive or passive-aggressive every time we'd converse over the next four years. At the time, I had no idea why she had such a growing animosity towards me. She'd intimidated me back into the freeze response so I couldn't think clearly.

XXX

I called her shortly after that last Mother's Day, thinking things were fine between us. Perhaps looking for a maternal response, I told her about a housemate who'd conned Predencia and myself out of money. (We didn't realise until we'd moved out.) We were due to go around his house to discuss the financial dispute later that night. I was anxious about the conversation and made the unfortunate mistake of telling her.

She became inexplicably aggressive. "You're no fucking Blakely if you let him take your money! You're no fucking Blakely!"

I was stunned by her anger and her demand that I stand up for myself when standing up for myself my whole life was never an option. (Standing up to her had just cost me two years of the silent treatment!)

I didn't know then, but she'd induced an emotional flashback. Not to any specific event, but to all the times she'd scared me with that growl. My heart was racing. I was dazed, confused, and so shocked by her response that I made a mental note never to look to her for reassurance again. And I didn't.

XXX

Despite being a bully towards me, she'd succeeded in convincing me that she was being taken advantage of by my younger sister. For the last five years, she'd told me she couldn't get her to leave her home. She wasn't contributing financially and wouldn't do anything around the house she said.

I'd gently encouraged her for years to assert herself, but she'd always say the conflict wasn't worth it. Her victim persona was Oscar-winning.

At about this time, my sister and I went to Ireland for a weekend to see some relatives. Shortly before the day of departure, I reassured her that I could talk to my sister on her behalf.

Again, I was shocked by the response. She growled at me in a threatening tone. "Don't you dare say anything! Don't you dare!" I persisted gently.

"Don't worry, Mum. It'll be fine."

She swore aggressively, making threats of what she would do if I followed through. Intimidated, I immediately backed down, trying to reassure her that, of course, I would respect her boundaries. My heart was racing, as I was still scared of her.

However, for the first time, in my mind, I questioned how she could be such a victim of my sister and yet be such a bully towards me. However, I had every intention of respecting her wishes.

## XXX

Despite being strategic, narcissists can often overplay their hands. If she hadn't been so aggressive towards me one last time, I might have kept my word.

My uncle had a pleasant conversation with her on the phone one day, then handed it to my sister, who declined to speak. So, I took the phone. I wasn't expecting any hostility because I'd already agreed to keep her confidence in our last conversation. Regardless, she asked questions like how was our holiday going, and what were we up to? But in a tone that was inappropriately abrasive for the questions she was asking. I was meek in response, answering her as quietly and as briefly as I could in an attempt not to provoke further aggression.

It occurred to me that her tone must have switched immediately from pleasant with my uncle to aggressive with me. My eyes started to open, and I began to see how devious she was.

It was only coming back on the plane that I suddenly got the urge to ask my sister the question I was told not to ask. I wanted to know what was beneath The Mother's confusing aggression. Within a few short moments, it was clear. Everything she'd told me was a lie, and she was terrified the truth would come out.

She needn't have been so fearful. Despite realising that she'd been lying to me for years, I never did confront her about it.

XXX

In our penultimate phone call, I stood up to her directly for only the second time in my life. She responded in typical fashion, shouting over me, swearing, and trying to guilt trip and shame me, telling me that she'd never be able to hold her head up in Ireland again. That my behaviour on holiday had embarrassed her that much.

She didn't allow me to explain myself, so for the first time, I told her "you're being rude". She continued to shout abuse over me.

I tried to maintain a degree of decorum by moving on to chit-chat as casually as I could, but she refused to play ball. So, I asked, "Do you not want me to talk anymore? Do you want to end the conversation here?" To which she aggressively growled, "Well, get on with it then! I can't stay on the phone listening to your fucking shit all day!"

Believe it or not, I tried to continue chit-chat after this, but she was monosyllabic in response, so I politely gave up and ended the call.

XXX

The reason she rang was that I'd had a couple (and I do mean only a couple) of glasses of wine in a restaurant with my sister and uncle. We all had wine. When I returned to my aunt's house later that night, I heard her complaining loudly to someone that I was 'sozzled!' "I can't understand a word she's saying. She's falling all over the place." I went to bed, angry at the lies I'd heard, but I didn't confront her. Scared that if I did, it would result in another lie, about how much I'd scared her with my confrontational drunken behaviour!

On leaving Ireland, she told me to write her and all my uncles individual thank you cards 'for being allowed to stay.' I probably would have written her a letter, thanking her for a nice stay, but being told to, made me not want to! I was 36 years old! I was also annoyed that my sister wasn't required to write a thank you card. So rightly or wrongly, I took the passive-aggressive route by taking my own sweet time. I sent sarcastically sickly-sweet cards three weeks later.

'Thank you so much for allowing me to stay with you. That was so kind of you! Thank you so much for eating dinner with me, spending time with me, and having conversations with me etc. etc. I will forever be indebted for your kindness.' (I don't remember it word for word, but that was the sentiment.)

Soon after I sent them, I got the phone call. My aunt complained to The Mother because I hadn't sent them immediately. And perhaps because she detected the sarcasm.

Simply put, she was raging because I'd had a drink with dinner and sent the thank you cards too late. This was the intolerable embarrassing behaviour I was so guilty of!

XXX

The dynamics are so deeply entrenched in the family that no one could see that I was being held to a different standard than my sister and uncle.

After I got over the shock of the call, I wrote The Mother a letter. It was respectful in tone, but I made it clear that if we were ever going to have a relationship, she couldn't speak to me the way she did. I said I wanted us to continue to have a relationship, but not like this. I have a right to say how I feel, just like she does.

I believed that she was so unreasonable on the phone because she was upset. I thought, with hindsight, when she'd calmed down, she'd be able to respond to the letter rationally. But she ignored it.

XXX

Three months after I sent it, she was 70. I was convinced to go along to the celebrations, much to my regret. Predencia and I travelled to Victoria station on a bitterly cold Saturday afternoon. My sisters, their partners, and The Mother greeted us in a busy pub. We all hoped for an appropriate response as she opened our present, a box of expensive jewellery. Instead, she said, "I'm not used to being treated so well!" My heart sank. I wanted to quip back, 'Never been treated so well?! I seem to remember taking you to Spain for a holiday one year, Mum, and that wasn't even a big one.' But something stopped me. Even though she likes to spoil special occasions, I don't.

So, I sat quietly, not saying anything. My older sister had to encourage her to wear the jewellery, as she wanted to put it back in the box.

We led her into the theatre next door to see the matinee of Billy Elliot. She complained to my younger sister, "Sure, this is old!" before promptly sleeping through the entire show. It transpired later that she'd been out till 3 am with her friends the night before. She didn't want to celebrate her birthday with us; she'd had the celebration that mattered last night.

After the show, we took her to dinner. Halfway through dinner, she gathered her belongings as if ready to leave. My older sister took charge again. "People are still eating, mum." She tried to scold her in a cajoling way. The Mother sat back down, smirking as if slightly embarrassed at being called out.

I tried to engage her in conversation throughout the evening. But to no avail.

"Did you enjoy the show?"

"Yes".

"Good. Which part was your favourite?"

"I don't know."

"Did you enjoy the food?"

"Yes".

"Good. What did you enjoy the most?"

"I don't know."

She sniggered her way through the one-sided conversation. On leaving the restaurant, as I went to say goodbye, she reached out her hand to shake mine. Something she'd never done before. I couldn't help but laugh. I was amused at her immaturity once again. I hugged her and kissed her on the cheek before turning to leave. At no point during her birthday celebration did she thank any of us.

XXX

Even after her disappointing behaviour on her 70th; after two years of the silent treatment; the spiteful Christmas card; using me to present a positive image to first my uncle; then her boyfriend; the abusive and accusatory phone call, and the ignoring of my letter; even after all that; I still naively thought that we could rebuild our relationship with new boundaries.

I set the bar as low to the ground as possible, due to her poor relationship skills. It was my dream to work towards the day that she would initiate contact with me on my birthday. If she was prepared to do this, I was willing to take responsibility for our relationship for the rest of the year. It would have been a significant breakthrough if she'd agreed to this. Imagine that! A once-a-year phone call as progress!

Two months later, it was my 37th. This was the first year I had the courage and strength not to call her on my birthday. Up until this year, I'd always made sure she'd have to acknowledge it because I'd call her.

There was no communication between us until five days later when she called me. Although I'd been feeling hurt for the last five days, the moment I saw her number ring, all the hurt disappeared. I was pleased she finally called and planned on taking this as my opportunity to set this new boundary.

Historically, on the rare occasion she initiated a phone call, it was like she wanted immediate compensation for making the effort. I could almost hear the cogs turning in her brain....'Well, I bothered to walk over to the phone, didn't I? I bothered to pick it up, didn't I? I bothered to dial the number, didn't I? I bothered to say 'Hello', didn't I? The very least you could do is all the work to make sure this interaction actually happens! I'm exhausted!'

This time was so very different. She was playing a character, acting out a script. I was immediately thrown, bamboozled, by a jolly and exuberant 'Happy Birthday!' (Something I believe she's never said to me before. I mean, never!)

I was caught in the double bind again. I could acknowledge reality and risk upsetting her or go along with her crazy-making game. Within seconds I decided to stay grounded in reality. However, I also wanted to give her the benefit of the doubt. Being well-trained in her micro aggressions, I knew that I had to tread carefully, or she would lash out. The Mother has very delicate sensibilities when it comes to her feelings. She rides roughshod over everyone else's, but hers are very precious indeed. This extreme sensitivity, combined with a callous disregard for other peoples' feelings, is another well-known trait that narcissists possess.

I tentatively said, "It was my birthday five days ago."

Long pause.

"Did you forget?" I asked timidly.

"No".

I scrambled around, trying to give her another get-out clause. "Were you busy?"

"No."

By my reasoning, if she'd forgotten or was too busy, that's forgivable. Instead of playing ball, she revealed herself, her true intent. She wanted me to know that she didn't forget and she wasn't busy. There was no valid reason other than she didn't want to acknowledge my birthday. She rang simply to check that I was hurt. She wanted to know that she'd hurt me because if I were affected emotionally by her behaviour, then that would mean she still had some control over me.

Suddenly, bizarrely, the insincere joyful tone became sarcastic, provoking and high-pitched. It's never taken much provocation to expose the mocking contempt lurking beneath the surface, so I'd heard something like this tone before, usually when she was mocking others. But nothing quite like this, directed squarely at me. It was as if she was acting badly. Trying to sound offended, but also goading me.

"Slapping me on the wrist, are we?! Slapping me on the

wrist?!" The cognitive dissonance her gear change caused left my heart pounding. Despite this, I tried to sound calm and assertive. "I'm not slapping you on the wrist. I'm just saying that my birthday was five days ago."

I'd spent my whole life trying to keep this monster at bay, and now I'd unleashed it. The no-win situation she'd set up for me was only going to make me feel either stupid or scared. This was the impossible, emotionally abusive choice presented to me.

Despite not feeling big or brave at that moment – I won. I witnessed the bizarre unravelling of a narcissist in all its glory. The moment she knew her power and control had slipped away, whilst she wasn't looking. Or, more likely, whilst she was enjoying punishing me with silence, keeping herself content by imagining how hurt I was. Completely unaware that I was no longer simply accepting her behaviour. I was now observing it, analysing it, and processing it.

I could feel her rage rising as she became aware..... Her reign is over. Because of her limited cognitive functioning, poor impulse control, rage and entitlement, she'd revealed her pettiness and lack of maturity with zero shame or awareness. I was punished for acknowledging the truth with another year of silence.

XXX

I'd resigned myself by this point that things were never going to get better between us. I was aware of what narcissism was by now, and it was clear that she was displaying every trait.

When I received a birthday card from her three weeks early the following year, I was amused at her efforts to demonstrate her contempt for me. She must have been sitting on this plan since our last phone call a year ago! Plotting how she could hurt me, even more this year. How could she demonstrate that she cares even less this time? A year of seething, just waiting for her moment to attack again.

I opened up the envelope immediately..... (I now knew that narcissists deliberately spoil special occasions for others, so I wasn't going to wait.)

Wow!....

If there was a competition for the world's most pointless card, this would have won. It was impossible to tell what gender, age group, or even what occasion it was for! I don't even think it could be called a card!

On the inside, 'Charlie'......' Mum'. Two words. I was quite impressed by the effort she must have gone through to find the world's most generic card ever. She must have trawled the shops for hours! Her poor feet!

A family member told me The Mother would be abroad for my birthday. So she wouldn't be able to phone, as she doesn't know how to use phones in that country! I deduced from this, and my early card that before getting on the plane, she also knew that she wouldn't know how to send mail from that country either!

This was the unbelievable explanation for why my pointless card arrived three weeks early and why I wouldn't hear from her on my birthday again.

Now that I was more grounded, less needy, and not so worried about her, she seemed to be wasting a lot of energy trying to get a reaction out of me. How could she do this whilst somehow looking innocent? She would have to concoct an elaborate scheme that would make her look innocent but stupid. (She often didn't mind looking stupid if it covered her tracks. She was even prone to say, 'Sure, I'm just a poor little Irish woman' when caught out in some scheme.)

She had nothing but time on her hands, so she took the time, effort and money to plot a scheme so elaborate as to seem ridiculous. I couldn't possibly accuse her of organising and paying for a holiday not to be around for my birthday. To have an alibi for why she could ignore my birthday again! That would be preposterous.

So incredible is the idea that I wouldn't dare confront her about it or tell anyone what I thought. I'd have to sit with the knowledge that I knew what she did. She knew what she did, and I knew she knew what she did. But I can't say a damn word because to say anything would be to accuse a dumb old lady of something petty and ridiculous, which might make me look petty and ridiculous, right?

XXX

I've frequently gone back and forth. I've hated her, been unable to forgive her, tried to be evolved enough to forgive her, and been furious with her for her limitations. However, the eventual undoing of our relationship was my gradual acceptance that she was unwilling to try to do better.

*One of the more infuriating traits of a narcissist is their compulsion to ruin special occasions.*

## Chapter 49 - Going No contact

Narcissists do not bend to reality. They do not learn from their mistakes. (Unless it suits them.) They do not grow. They do not self-reflect. (Unless self-aware, which is rare).

Once I'd wrapped my head around the fact that almost everything is planned, that life is a play, or a chess board, to the narcissist; once I understood that almost everything is calculated, contrived; that the outcome is almost always pre-determined, I saw no choice but to go 'no contact.'

It became a battle for myself or her. I questioned, did I need this person in my life so much as to allow the toxicity to go unchallenged, or did I choose freedom, happiness and truth?

I chose the latter.

By 38, I'd finally accepted that the relationship was not real. I'd made it all up. I finally understood that she was too broken. There would never be any healing or honesty or change in her. She'd decided long ago that nothing would break her. Nothing would melt her heart. She was not open to receiving, ever.

I ended my contact with her in a 12-page letter. I didn't mention anything about my childhood or teens. I wrote from when our relationship began its apparent demise after I'd told her that she wasn't emotionally supportive.

I finally told her how ridiculous her behaviour was, how I knew her motives, and how I knew she didn't love me. I expressed compassion for her childhood and said that no one deserved the childhood she'd had. I told her I loved her, but the relationship was too damaging to me. I'd done everything I could to fix it and finally accepted its ending. I said that I would like her to respect my boundaries for once. She'd had ample opportunity to communicate with me over the years but had refused to do so. Therefore, I was now over it. I didn't expect anything from her, not even a Christmas card. I said that if she tried to contact me after this letter, she'd prove me right, that she doesn't respect me or care about how I feel.

I didn't want to regret anything, so I removed some swear words here and there, and softened the tone before I posted it. I wanted to be as honest as I could whilst maintaining respect for her.

As I posted the letter, my heart was pounding. It felt exhilarating to say what I had to say, and it felt empowering to let the relationship go. But I was also shit scared at the same time!

A couple of days later, the phone rang late one morning. I panicked, immediately knowing it was her. When I got up later that morning, I dialled 1471 to find that it was. She hadn't called that line in years!

Even though I knew she had inherent disrespect for me, I was still shocked at this behaviour. All the time I tried so hard to have a relationship with her, she was rejecting and dismissive. In response to me saying, 'please respect my boundaries and don't' call', she calls!.....Several times!........ Then tried to use my sister as a flying monkey to guilt-trip me into seeing her. (All textbook).

I was told that The Mother was crying hysterically and that it was most likely a 'wake-up call' for her. I didn't buy it. I'd done enough research on narcissism to know that she was reacting very predictably.

As a result of my letter, The Mother invited me, through my sister, to a pub with my other sister. She thought it would be a good idea to have a very difficult private conversation, in public,....with alcohol, with my other sister present, to muddy the waters.

I didn't know it then, but she wanted a public meeting with my sister because she was scared of having a private 1-2-1 with me.

My sister said that The Mother didn't agree with some things in my letter. I suddenly realised the reason for the invitation. She wanted to have the last word. That's all.

Since she'd had free reign to say precisely what she thought and felt about me for 38 years, I thought, 'no. I don't want to give you a platform to respond because you have nothing new to say, and this relationship is beyond the point of repair, so there's no point.'

Because I'd refused to meet with her, I got a nine-page, vitriolic letter full of half-truths, manipulations and distortions, ending with, 'You are no longer my daughter'. Isn't that a bit like handing in your resignation after you've been sacked?!

It's common for narcissists to take a grain of truth and twist it into a lie. These lies are the most difficult to defend against because of the grain of truth embedded within them.

The gist of the letter was that she'd always been a wonderful, kind mother, and I'd always been a selfish, lazy, ungrateful daughter. (Again, very predictable.) One example of her wonderfulness was that she bought me a bus pass when I was 12 years old!

She did buy me a bus pass when I was 12 but wasn't that her responsibility as a parent? Was I supposed to go out and work to buy my bus pass for school at 12 years old? She sent me to a school outside my catchment area for selfish reasons. Twenty-six years later, she used it as an example of what a wonderful parent she was. Because she'd paid for my travel to school?!

This is how petty and small-minded these people are. Whatever money they spend will be used as a tool for leverage when the time is right.

XXX

The Mother had always spoken of her childhood and broken

marriage with rage. My desperation to bond with her seemed to bring up similar feelings. It was clear what her story was. 'Men are bastards. Love isn't real. It doesn't exist'. She angrily told herself this story on a loop daily, increasing her fury, looking for clues and examples to prove her right. She didn't get that validation from me because the more she rejected me, the harder I tried. Only when I finally gave up did I imagine she felt a sense of triumph.

'Aha! I knew it! Just as I'd suspected all along! She never loved me! She was pretending. Well, boy, am I glad I never responded to all those times she tried to show me love! I knew she'd reveal her true self one day. It took 38 years, but I was right!'

She 'won' in the end, as far as she's concerned. Of course, she didn't win. If she'd allowed herself to lower her defences just a little; if the storyline of being a self-sacrificing mother to a useless daughter hadn't been so important, my love could have made a positive difference to her life, like Predencia's made to mine.

She never understood that her story became a self-fulfilling prophecy by resisting change. Or maybe she did understand this, and perhaps that was the point.

The narrative is more important to a narcissist than happiness because they do not see happiness as anything other than having their story validated. Even though they know, it's not true!

XXX

I've now let go of my anger and frustration towards The Mother. Despite finally being free of her, the legacy of having an NPD parent is that I've increasingly struggled with my physical health due to my chosen coping strategy. The emotional abuse I'd tolerated my whole life was now damaging my physical health.

By 36, I started to display the first signs of alcohol abuse, with raised cholesterol. Because the NHS didn't connect the dots, I've never been offered appropriate treatment. The NHS has been ineffective at connecting the dots between mental and physical health for a long time. The nurse told me to exercise more and eat more healthily. I was fit because I ran regularly and didn't have an excessively fatty diet. I knew what the problem was, but she didn't ask. Instead, she stuck to her script.

At 40, my doctor's notes describe 'depression relating to ongoing difficulties with the Mother and an emotionally deprived and abused childhood. Tried to break with mum two years ago.'

Any doctor who read this could have thought this was suggestive of the trauma bond, but no one did.

By 43, my bile duct was inflamed.

By 46, the renal cortex of my kidneys was thinning.

By 48, I was experiencing alcoholic neuropathy – tingling in the extremities due to nerve damage.

By 49, my ankles and feet were swollen, making walking painful – an early symptom of kidney failure.

No doctor ever informed me of these diagnoses. I only discovered them by reading my doctor's notes years later and doing my own research.

*The nine diagnosable traits for Narcissistic Personality Disorder from the DSM-V at the time of going to print are:*

- *A grandiose sense of self-importance*

- *A preoccupation with fantasies of unlimited success, power, brilliance, beauty or ideal love*

- *A belief that they are special or unique and can only be understood by or should associate with other special or high-status people or institutions*

- *A need for excessive admiration*

- *A sense of entitlement*

- *Interpersonally exploitative behaviour*
- *A lack of empathy*
- *Envy of others or a belief that others are envious of them*
- *A demonstration of arrogant and haughty behaviours or attitudes**

# Chapter 50 - Complex Post Traumatic Stress Disorder (CPTSD)

There are several common reactions to narcissistic abuse. Some 'fight types' become narcissists themselves, others become OCD-type perfectionists, and some become avoidant. All these responses can be damaging in their own way. For example, the narcissist is perpetually disappointed in others. The OCD type finds it hard to be vulnerable, making intimacy difficult. Whilst the avoidant type is very alone in the world.

I believe that CPTSD is the most self-destructive response to narcissistic abuse. However, because it is so painful, it is also the response that will most likely activate a soul-searching focus on recovery.

I discovered that I had CPTSD about five years after discovering that The Mother was a narcissist. I was 43 years old. This was another pivotal moment in my journey towards healing because I could finally understand my symptoms and how to reduce them. It was also crucial for my growth to move away from the obsession of trying to understand her and turn my attention towards self-care.

XXX

Complex Post Traumatic Stress Disorder (CPTSD) is more complex and, therefore, more challenging to treat than Post

Traumatic Stress Disorder (PTSD).

Because PTSD can happen at any time in life, after a one-time event, such as a mugging for example; it tends to be more immediately recognisable as a mental health problem. It can therefore be picked up relatively quickly. The symptoms are recognisably distinct from our personalities.

Not so with CPTSD, which usually develops after ongoing trauma. If trauma is persistent throughout childhood, CPTSD will interfere with the formation of the personality. It will become infused and develop alongside the personality, making it indistinguishable. Simply put, CPTD appears to be who we are.

Suppose CPTSD develops in adulthood, after an abusive relationship, for example. In that case, I imagine there is more of a chance of noticing what's happening, so help may be sought earlier than if it develops in childhood.

### Symptoms of CPTSD

In recent years, the list of symptoms for CPTSD has become so long as to become unhelpful. With such a long list, almost anyone could say they have some form of CPTSD. So, I will stick to the five main symptoms I know I had. The five symptoms I came across when I first heard of CPTSD:

**A Vicious Inner Critic**
**Self-Abandonment**
**Toxic Shame**
**Emotional Flashbacks**
**Social Anxiety**

**A Vicious Inner Critic** – This is our internal monologue. Which we all have, but the sufferer of CPTSD has an internal monologue that is vicious towards the self. We've heard the mantras from our abuser so many times that we now internalise their voice. They no longer need to be present or alive to continue their abuse. Their mantras are now inside us. We've turned on our inner child, just like our parents turned on us when we were children (if the CPTSD results from parental abuse.)

CBT is probably most beneficial for initially tackling this Vicious Inner Critic, in my opinion. It's an excellent place to start because once the power of the Vicious Inner Critic is reduced, we create space to bring in the opposite. An inner nurturing parent who will teach us self-compassion. Once we've tamed the inner critic, meditation is a good practice to follow on from CBT, as it provides us with a deeper self-awareness.

**Self-Abandonment** – This is the behaviour that manifests as a result of the Vicious Inner Critic. People with CPTSD can be easily guilt-tripped and shamed into serving the needs of others, even to the detriment of their own needs.

'Repetition Compulsion' is another reason victims of narcissists self-abandon. We're caught up in getting the narcissist to emotionally give us what we need from them.

In hindsight, I believe self-abandonment is at least one reason I chose to pursue drama and teaching. I wasn't making decisions based on who I was. I was basing them on becoming the person I wanted to be. I could become an extrovert, a show-off, a public speaker and enjoy it just by repetition and trying hard. With my choices, I was subconsciously recreating the situation I was forced to endure at home. Whilst teaching or acting, I couldn't flee or publicly get upset or angry with myself – just like I never could with The Mother. I had no choice but to stay and endure her abuse silently, just like I had no choice but to continue acting or teaching whilst enduring an emotional flashback. This is the 'freeze' response that entraps us.

**Toxic Shame**- Is the core wound of emotional abandonment. Unlike healthy shame, which can help us to make morally acceptable decisions, toxic shame is debilitating because it is not ours. It is a shame our abuser has projected onto us, and it often stops us from getting help.

If our abusers could feel shame, they wouldn't have

committed the abuse they did. It would have stopped them. But because they can't feel their shame, it becomes a burden the victim carries. Like social anxiety, toxic shame keeps us isolated and lonely, and the abuser safe from reprisals.

**Emotional Flashbacks** - Until we understand emotional flashbacks, we think we're reacting to a current event rather than being triggered by it. So we scold ourselves for over or under reacting, not understanding that our inner child has been activated and is reacting.

Emotional flashbacks are hard to recognise initially, especially if we've been suffering from them our whole life because they become deeply embedded in our personalities over time.

A simple way to recognise them is to become more present to our inner world. This helps us get better at recognising when we've been triggered. The more inner child work we do, the more s/he will become real, and the more s/he will learn to trust us.

**Social Anxiety/Social Phobia** – Social anxiety in its extremes can lead to social phobia, resulting in avoidance of social interactions. What's behind social anxiety is a fear of rejection and a fear of being mocked and ridiculed. We fear not being accepted by others. That if others knew who we are, they wouldn't like us. This intense fear of being exposed as fundamentally flawed and unlovable leads to a life of solitude, isolation and loneliness, which can eventually result in depression, and even suicide.

In my teens, I read books on overcoming social anxiety and shyness, determined to overcome these afflictions. But nothing helped. The more I focussed on them, the more obsessed I became with wanting to be rid of these traits, the more these traits became a problem.

As a teenager, I believed my shyness was something I'd grow out of. I believed that if I just got on with things; forced myself to do the things I wished I could do, a kind of do-it-yourself exposure therapy, I'd be healed.

I didn't understand that the social anxiety came from a deeper toxic shame. I didn't understand that by throwing myself into the lion's den, as it were, of uncomfortable situations, I was self-abandoning. In the process, I was creating even deeper, longer-lasting psychological wounds and distressing physiological symptoms. I didn't understand that I was choosing to put myself into situations that would inevitably cause emotional flashbacks, which would induce further toxic shame, followed by self-abandonment. So, I continued with the subconscious negative self- perpetuating cycle, unaware of the trauma I was continuing to cause myself.

*The good news is that there is an abundance of self-help tools to support us in our recovery from narcissistic abuse. We don't need to wait for a formal diagnosis for them or us. We can empower ourselves by trying various tools and then honing in on what feels most beneficial.*

## Chapter 51 - Moving On

I finally realised how The Mother succeeded in getting away with the abuse she perpetrated, without me even knowing I was a victim. She protected herself by manipulating me into doing to myself what she wanted to do to me. This way, her hands remained clean.

She didn't starve me, but she convinced me that I was fat and gave the impression that I'd have a chance of being loved by her if I lost weight. Then did nothing as I starved myself.

She didn't beat me, but conditioned me to hate myself. Then did nothing, as I developed a self-harming habit.

She didn't attempt to murder me, but she told me she'd prefer it if I were dead. Then did nothing as I tried to take my life several times.

Why would a narcissist sabotage the life and happiness of another? Envy. They must destroy whatever someone else has, whether it's health, beauty or confidence. Positive traits in another makes a narcissist feel insecure. So, they must take down another to restore their equilibrium.

XXX

The most challenging aspect of narcissistic abuse to recover from for me was the trauma bond. Despite there being no contact between us for 11 years, I still thought about her every day.

XXX

So, how do we deal with the narcissist in our life? The advice I came across was to run. Run for the hills, and don't look back! Go, no contact. But this isn't for everyone. What if the narcissist is the co-parent of our young children? Or our mother/father-in-law or boss? Well, then the advice is to 'grey rock'. As in, be as interesting as a grey rock, because expressing anger doesn't work. Neither does trying to reconcile. They will never hear our side, not with empathy anyway. So, we need to act like we have nothing to give, around the narcissist. We need to pretend that we're empty. Only then will they leave us in peace, because we're boring without the drama of us trying to connect with them. They still need to get their supply from somewhere, though.

The caveat is that initially, our disinterest may spur them on to pursue us with more vengeance. The Mother ghosted me for five years, on and off, when I was trying to establish a respectful relationship. But as soon as she received the no-contact letter, it was like a moth to a flame!

'No contact' or 'low contact' with 'grey rocking' is the only wise choice when dealing with a narcissist. Anything else gives supply, and when we give supply, we deplete our energy.

We must stay strong, whatever the choice we make. They'll quickly run out of steam if they don't have our energy to feed off, in my experience.

.

XXX

She threatened suicide the day my sister was due to leave her house, after a short stay, in to move into her own. She was so distressed by the idea of my sister's independence that she demanded to be admitted to a psych ward. Then demanded less than 24hrs later to be discharged, when she realised that psychiatric care wasn't a bunch of women sitting around crocheting and drinking endless cups of tea all day. (To be discharged, she had to admit that she said she was suicidal for attention.)

She's become a regular emergency services caller, and has seen many heart specialists because she believes she has heart issues. (It's possible that her FDIA –Fictitious Disorder Imposed on Another has morphed into a Fictitious Disorder because she no longer has anyone to project it onto.)

After much wasting of resources, all the experts have agreed that she has a healthy heart and is most likely experiencing panic attacks. I don't know whether she's faking panic attacks for attention or genuinely having panic attacks. Either way, there is no physical health problem.

XXX

I've cried a lot of tears throughout my recovery process. That's ok; tears are healing. They help us release the trauma locked within us.

After the tears came the anger. For the first time, a healthy anger that was directed at the person responsible for my pain. When I went through this phase, I wanted to take her to court and see justice. But time and karma serve up a particular kind of justice. It took years to move from anger and rage, which felt scary sometimes, to a calm acceptance of what was.

XXX

Our worlds collided for the last time when I recently attended my uncle's funeral. (The one who drove me home from school when I had food poisoning.) She cried when she saw me. She put her arms out for me to hug her – something she'd never done before; and said she was 'very sorry if' she'd 'ever said or done anything to offend' me. It was a hollow apology. She had no idea what she was apologising for, and if we were to get into it, I'm sure she'd have gone into defence mode and taken it back. But I wasn't interested in rehashing anything, and it wasn't the time or the place, so I thanked her.

She spent the whole time trying to connect with me. She even complimented my appearance for the first time, marvelling at 'how young' I looked. (It's hard to believe it was a sincere compliment, but it was nice to hear nonetheless.) I was polite but distant in response.

On leaving, she asked for my address. It was a strange experience. All the pain and anger I'd carried around for years disappeared instantly.

Sometime later, she sent me some money. I was grateful for it and expressed this to her, as it did make a difference in my life. (I managed to get some dental work I'd needed for a long time, and Predencia and I enjoyed our anniversary on her.)

I was aware, however, that this was simply a manoeuvre to gain control. She knew that I no longer feared her and that I was no longer manipulated by her tears. The last and only way she could feel superior to me was for me to be indebted to her.

I'm aware of the psychology behind her giving. I therefore cannot be controlled by it. I can feel and express gratitude, which I have done, but I don't feel I owe her anything in return.

### XXX

Being raised by a narcissistic parent has been described by some as similar to being in a cult. It should be no surprise, then, that in my quest for freedom, I ran from The Mother straight into the arms of a cult. It took me 12 years to escape it.

The great benefit of having deprogrammed myself from brainwashing (twice now) is that I've developed an inbuilt gaslighting detector. I can now see that narcissism is everywhere.

### XXX

The Mother frequently said that all she wanted was four children. I could never understand how she could have parented so badly if it was her dream to be a parent. As an adult, I suspect that she decided to have children simply because she knew it was the only way she could control others. She wasn't innovative enough or influential enough to succeed in the workplace, so she created an environment where she could be the boss. Where she could dominate.

I believe that more intelligent narcissists gravitate towards positions of power, like politics; and of course, places where they are the centre of attention, like the performing arts. There is also a worrying trend of narcissists working within the mental health field.

I don't think it's an accident that, at least in the UK, narcissism is not included in the curriculum of a psychology degree. The result is that it's common for mental health workers, even professionals within the NHS, to know little to nothing about NPD.

I believe that narcissists infiltrate mental health services, just like paedophiles infiltrate places of work with children. Once narcissists get into positions of power within mental health services, they can ensure that narcissism goes unchallenged because exposing it would be dangerous for them. By being in positions of power, they can control the flow of information.

Once the cat's out of the bag, once everyone knows what narcissism is, what the traits are and what the ramifications are for victims, the game is up. They've lost.

XXX

Rich and powerful narcissists aren't going to try to figure out how to make the world a better place for everyone. Their very nature determines that their focus will be on self-interest. 'The old boys club.' We need to open our eyes. They're all around us.

Is it an accident that the DSM-V (the gold standard for mental health diagnosis) is so vague and unhelpful regarding the symptoms of NPD?

For example, how do we diagnose 'A preoccupation with fantasies of unlimited success, power, brilliance, beauty or ideal love'?

A narcissist would need to be honest about their fantasies to be diagnosed. Is a narcissist likely to be honest about these fantasies? Perhaps a grandiose narcissist might. A covert narcissist? Highly unlikely.

*How is a narcissist expected to be honest when they operate from a 'false self? (A character they've created to get through life.)And who decides what traits should go in the DSM-V, and why? These are important questions to ask, I think.*

# Chapter 52 – Recovery tools and tips

It's hard to find mental health professionals within the NHS who have extensive knowledge of NPD, and its link to reactive disorders in others such as CPTSD, Depression, Anxiety, Eating Disorders, Suicide, Addictions, OCD etc. Most have never heard of Matrix Re-imprinting, either.

It's likely that even if we're fortunate enough to secure therapy within the NHS, we may be disappointed with the results.

Complex Post Traumatic Stress Disorder is now more widely diagnosed, but the therapy offered is limited and hard to access. However, in the UK, the NHS is the only option for therapy for some of us, so I'd like to guide you.

XXX

A GP visit is no longer needed in the first instance when accessing mental health support.

An online self-referral form can be filled in (for Time to Talk, Health in Mind or a Wellbeing Service), after which short-term online CBT (Cognitive Behavioural Therapy) will be the most likely option offered.

Access to longer-term and more intensive therapies can be gained through hoop-jumping into secondary mental health services. However, the waiting lists are long.

Anyone self-medicating with alcohol or other substances will likely be rejected from mental health services and redirected to an addiction service, where the support is usually not psychologically informed. Of course, it makes no sense to demand a person get rid of their coping strategy before giving them better ones; and it makes no sense to provide addiction support that is not psychologically informed when the original trauma is psychological. However, that is how the topsy-turvy system currently runs.

XXX

With all the challenges above, it's understandable that those who can afford it would take the private route. However, even if a knowledgeable professional can be found outside the NHS, traditional psychology/counselling is unaffordable to most at £50+ per weekly session.

Having said this, I believe each branch of therapy has its value. Psychodynamic counselling (talking therapy) is an excellent first stage for those that have never been allowed to speak up.

**CBT** is an excellent tool to help us untangle ourselves from negative and destructive repetitive thought patterns.

**EMDR,** (Eye Movement Desensitisation and Reprocessing) **EFT** (Emotional Freedom Technique) and **Matrix Re-imprinting** are all helpful to various degrees in helping us to overcome PTSD/CPTSD and childhood trauma.

I'd like to share some other options from charities and funded organisations.

Some are **MIND** (the biggest national mental health charity in the UK), The National Association for People Abused in Childhood (**NAPAC**), and **24-hour mental health lines** via 111.

Another source of support is local support groups, usually free. As are online support forums. Narcissistic abuse recovery programmes have also popped up in the last few years. These are most likely not free.

Another way of empowering ourselves during the recovery process is to do research. Knowledge is power, and there are various sources of information: websites, YouTube Vloggers, Books, Documentaries and Self-Healing Tools.

Below are two of the most useful websites that benefitted me during my recovery.

**daughtersofnarcissisticmothers.com** – Despite some controversy over whether the creator of this site is a narcissist herself, the website itself is a great free resource. And has the best description of a narcissistic mother that I could find. (Better than the DSM-V!)

**psychforums.com**- (The Narcissistic Personality Disorder section.) This site is useful for getting the inside scoop on how narcissists feel. There are several self-aware narcissists out there, and because of the site's anonymity, they can sometimes be very helpful in answering questions. (However, they can get agitated with survivors of narcissistic abuse, and will sometimes tell victims/survivors to go elsewhere for support. That this is their forum. Nonetheless, it makes for another useful, empowering source of free information.

Finally, in the last few years, there have been a variety of useful vloggers on YouTube. Some professional, some self-aware narcissists, and some recovered victims. A few of my favourites are:

**Lisa A Romano** – Life Coach and author – Her focus is helping victims understand the narcissists' behaviour.

Zoe from **Live Abuse Free** uploads videos analysing people's behaviour in the public domain. An easy and very interesting way of breaking down what can sometimes feel like inaccessible, hard-to-grasp information.

**Dr Ramani** – Clinical Psychologist. She has the same aim as Lisa but has a very different energy. Both are useful and interesting in their unique way.

**Richard Grannon** – In recovery from CPTSD. It's valuable to hear from someone who has made significant progress in their recovery.

**Lee Hammock** – Diagnosed with Narcissistic Personality Disorder. He uses his past behaviour to explain the thinking process of a narcissist.

**HG Tudor** – Another self-aware narcissist uses his experience to educate others. He has also written books on the subject.

**Sam Vaknin** - Professor, psychologist and author. A self-aware covert narcissist.

Books that have helped me in my recovery are:

**The Mythology of Self Worth** by Richard L Franklin– the book that changed my life

**Children of Emotionally Immature Parents** by Lyndsay C Gibson – A great book that can give some much-needed perspective on our parents' maladaptive behaviours

**CPTSD – From Surviving to Thriving** by Pete Walker – For understanding our trauma from a deeper perspective

**Matrix Re-imprinting using EFT** by Karl Dawson & Sasha Allenby – A good tool if Matrix re-imprinting therapy is too expensive

**Toxic Parents** by Susan Foreward – Offers compassionate guidance on how to detach from toxic parents

**Healing the shame that binds you** – John Bradshaw – A guide to understanding the complexity of toxic shame

**Getting the love you want** – Harville Hendrix – Great for traumatised adults who want to learn how to do healthy relationships

**The Road Less Travelled** by M. Scott Peck – A good first book on the road to recovery

**The Power of Now** by Eckhart Tolle – A more spiritual guide to recovery

**You can heal your life** – Louise L Hay – An empowering book about the power of self-healing

**The Assertive Woman** by Nancy Austin and Stanlee Phelps – Offers practical tips for how to exercise assertiveness in our lives.

Understanding the theory of narcissism and complex post-traumatic stress disorder is a necessary part of our healing but getting ourselves professional 1-2-1 help is also essential.

Talking therapy is an excellent release for those who've never felt listened to or understood. It's important to build a rapport with a therapist that validates you.

Matrix Re-imprinting is a good follow-on from talking therapy, and it's comparable to other, more traditional talking therapies at about the £50ph mark. It can work relatively fast, so it is good value for money. We can do sessions further apart than talking therapy, keeping costs down. (I used to have once-a-month sessions until I felt far enough into my recovery to have one-off sessions. Which are useful when new triggers surface.)

As part of the healing process, I became interested in holistic health. I realised I had no idea how to care for myself physically, mentally or emotionally. And all of this self-neglect is interlinked. The following documentaries series' whet the appetite for holistic health and can be found on Netflix.

**Heal, Goop,** and **What the Health?**

XXX

The last part of the jigsaw was finding a spiritual dimension to life. I developed a belief that the purpose of my life was to grow and learn, and transform the pain of my earlier life into something that could benefit others.

I believe that we all have a divine purpose in life. We all came here, born into this time and place, to our parents for a specific reason. We all have only a mission we can fulfil. And nobody has a right to interrupt that mission, even if they brought us into the world.

I believe that each of us has a personal responsibility to figure out what our mission or divine purpose is. When we're on the right track, the universe, or God, whichever you choose to believe in, will let us know.

We don't need to ascribe to any conventional religion to find a spiritual dimension to our life. We can discover our spiritual self through a variety of secular ways if that is our preference.

Discovering a spiritual aspect of ourselves can be done through Daily Positive Affirmations of ('I deserve.....'), Breath Work, Meditation, Mindfulness, EFT (Emotional Freedom Technique), Acupressure, Crystals, Tai Chi, Yoga (Kundalini), Essential oils: (Lavender Oil for depression and Jasmine for anxiety.) CBD oil (there are proven varied benefits to both physical and mental health, particularly anxiety and depression. Try more organic medicinal versions online rather than shop-bought or flavoured ones.) Outdoor exercise such as walking, jogging or cycling helps release endorphins, particularly in scenic surroundings. A combination of group activity with solo work is also good. Lastly, nutrition deserves a mention. I'd recommend attempting to 'grow your own'. We can start small with just one plant. Aside from the benefits of eating organic and cheaper foods, gardening is therapeutic and empowering.

XXX

All of the strategies above can be researched online easily. Most will have free tutorials on YouTube. Learning these skills is usually cheap, if not free.

Due diligence is, of course, encouraged. These are just my opinions based on personal experience. I'M NOT A DOCTOR AND HAVE NO MEDICAL TRAINING, SO I'M NOT SUGGESTING STOPPING ANY MEDICATION, AND I WOULDN'T KNOW WHAT THE EFFECTS OF MIXING OILS WITH PRESCRIPTIONS ARE.

Just a quick note on due diligence. I would advise always taking the extra few minutes to research the researchers. Many vloggers and content creators provide links to the research they've shared. So, viewers can verify the validity of the study themselves.

I recommend making at least one of the recovery tools above a part of daily practice. (It doesn't need to be the same activity every day. A variety is better.) That way, recovery becomes assimilated into our life rather than being a compartmentalised activity.

As they say in AA, take the best, and leave the rest. Recovery is a long journey with no end destination, just like the pursuit of happiness.

*Enjoy the process, have patience, and know that there is always work to be done, if we want to continually evolve to be the very best that we can be.*

'The truth shall set you free'
John 8:32

Please consider rating this book if you enjoyed it; and leaving a review on social media if possible; but preferably on Amazon.